go getter 3

Students' Book

Sandy Zervas with Catherine Bright

Contents

Grammar/Communication video | Grammar animation | Culture video

Contents

0 Get started!

He usually wins! I can use the Present Simple.

In this unit

Vocabulary
- Places in town
- Means of transport
- Jobs
- School subjects
- Places in a school
- Adjectives
- Adjectives with prepositions
- Food and drink
- Containers

Grammar
- Present Simple
- Adverbs of frequency
- Question words
- *be going to*
- Countable and uncountable nouns, *some* and *any*

1 0.1 Intro Video

Hello!

George: Hi, I'm George Nichols. Nice to meet you. This is my brother, Harry.
Harry: Unfortunately. Hi, everyone. I'm thirteen years old and George is fourteen.
George: We live in London with our parents. That's our mum.
Mum: Hi, I'm Angela.
Harry: And this is our dad, Peter. Dad and I love sports.
Dad: That's right. We often play tennis together. He usually wins!
George: Harry is a tennis genius.
Harry: Thank you.
George: And I'm just … a genius!
Harry: He thinks he's funny!
George: At least you're never bored with me! We often hang out with Emma. Emma is our cousin. She lives with our gran.

Emma: Oh, hello there! I'm Emma.
Poppy: And I'm Poppy. Emma and I are best friends.
Emma: We're thirteen years old and we go to school together.
Poppy: We usually go by bike.
Emma: And sometimes we go by car, Gran drives us when we're really late!
Gran: Emma, your helmet!
Emma: Thanks, Gran. This is my gran, Bertie.
Gran: Hello.
Emma: She's the best granny in the world! She always makes pancakes for breakfast!
Poppy: Emma! Let's go!
Emma: OK. See you later!

1 1 1.2 Watch or listen and read. Is Harry good at tennis? Does George like making jokes? Are Emma and Poppy cousins? What does Emma have for breakfast?

2 Work in pairs.
Student A: Read out a line from the dialogue.
Student B: Guess who said it.
Then swap roles.

Grammar Present Simple

+	–
I/You/We/They **play** tennis.	I/You/We/They **don't play** tennis.
He/She/It **plays** tennis.	He/She/It **doesn't play** tennis.
?	**Short answers**
Do I/you/we/they **play** tennis?	Yes, I/you/we/they **do**. No, I/you/we/they **don't**.
Does he/she/it **play** tennis?	Yes, he/she/it **does**. No, he/she/it **doesn't**.

3 **Complete the sentences with the correct form of the Present Simple. Cross out the days when the people are busy. When are they all free?**

Monday Tuesday Wednesday
~~Thursday~~ Friday Saturday Sunday

1 Mr Nichols and Harry *play* (play) tennis on Thursdays.
2 Emma has dance classes twice a week. She ________ (not have) them on Mondays, Wednesdays, Thursdays or at the weekend.
3 George ________ (do) karate on Tuesdays.
4 Mrs Nichols and Gran ________ (not go) to the gym on Tuesdays, Wednesdays, Fridays or Sundays.
5 Harry ________ (have) tennis practice on Tuesdays, Thursdays, Saturdays and Sundays.
6 Poppy ________ (not go) to art class on Tuesdays, Wednesdays, Thursdays, Fridays or at the weekend.

4 1.3 **Listen and repeat. Which places do you visit for fun?**

Vocabulary Places in town

bank café cinema hospital hotel museum
park restaurant stadium theatre

5 **Complete the sentences with the places in the Vocabulary box.**

1 George and his dad go to the *stadium* to watch the football.
2 Emma and Poppy ride their bikes in the ________ .
3 Mr Nichols is a doctor. He works at a ________ .
4 After the gym, Gran and Mrs Nichols have coffee at a ________ .
5 At the weekend, Harry goes to the ________ to see a film.

6 1.4 **Listen and repeat. Which means of transport can you see in the photo on page 4?**

Vocabulary Means of transport

bike boat bus car motorbike
plane taxi train tram underground

7 **How do the people travel? In your notebook, write questions and answers. Then act out the dialogues in pairs.**

1

2

3

4

5

1 Emma / go to her dance class / bike?
A: *Does Emma go to her dance class by bike?*
B: *No, she doesn't. She goes by bus.*
2 Harry and George / go to school / car?
3 Mr Nichols / go to the hospital / underground?
4 Emma and Gran / travel to France / train?
5 Mrs Nichols / go to work / taxi?

Grammar Adverbs of frequency

	Adverb + verb
■■■■ always	I **always go** to school by bike.
■■■□ usually	
■■□□ often	**Adverb + to be**
■□□□ sometimes	I **am never** late for school.
□□□□ never	

8 **Find all the sentences with adverbs of frequency in the dialogue on page 4.**

9 **Write five true sentences about yourself. Use adverbs of frequency and words from the Vocabulary boxes.**

I always go to the park with my friends on Saturdays.

Emma's uncle

Poppy: Who is that man in the photo?
Emma: That's my Uncle Eric in his studio.
Poppy: His studio? What does he do?
Emma: Look at the painting, Poppy! He's an artist.
Poppy: Cool! I'd love to see his work. Where does he live?
Emma: In Madrid. His wife, Eva, is Spanish.
Poppy: How often do they come to the UK?
Emma: They usually visit us in the summer. Uncle Eric says Spain's too hot in August.
Poppy: I love Spain!
Emma: Here's an idea – let's visit Uncle Eric and Aunt Eva in Madrid! They always ask me and Gran to go. Plus, Aunt Eva's a brilliant chef! She has her own restaurant.
Poppy: Yes, please! When can we go?

1 Read the dialogue. Complete the sentences with one word in each gap.

1 The man in the photo is an *artist* .
2 Emma's uncle lives in ________ .
3 Emma's ________ Eva is Spanish.
4 Eva works in a ________ .

2 1.5 Listen and repeat. Does anyone in your family do one of these jobs?

Vocabulary Jobs

artist builder bus driver chef doctor farmer footballer nurse office worker pilot police officer shop assistant singer teacher vet

3 In pairs, answer the questions. In which jobs do people:

1 work outdoors?
builder, bus driver, …
2 work indoors?
3 work with children?
4 work with animals?
5 help other people?

Grammar Question words

How What Where When Who

4 A friend is interviewing Harry about his dad's job for a school project. Complete the questions with a question word.

1 *What* does your dad do?
2 ________ does he work?
3 ________ does he wear at work?
4 ________ does he start work?
5 ________ does he travel to work?

5 Look at the factfile and find the answers to the questions from Exercise 4. Ask and answer the questions in pairs.

Peter Nichols

Job: *doctor*
Works at: *Park Hill General Hospital*
Wears: *white coat*
Starts work: *usually at 8 a.m.*
Travels to work: *by motorbike*

A: *What does Harry's dad do?*
B: *He's a doctor.*

6 In pairs, interview each other.

Student A: Imagine you do one of the jobs in the Vocabulary box.
Student B: Prepare an empty factfile for Student A like the one in Exercise 5.
Ask questions and complete the file.
Student A: Answer Student B's questions. Then swap roles.

B: *What do you do?*
A: *I'm a …*

I'm going to ...

This year, I'm going to study Geography more. I'm going to get straight As! I'm also going to use the school library more often.

My parents are going to buy me my own laptop! I'm very excited! I'm going to use it in my Art projects!

I'm going to stop taking my brother's school things without asking. He gets really mad when I take his P.E. bag!

This year, I'm going to get up earlier in the morning. I'm also going to make healthy choices at the school canteen!

1 **Read what Emma, Poppy, George and Harry say. Match their names to photos A–D.**

A  B 

C  D 

A – *George*

2 1.6 **Listen and repeat. Which are your favourite school subjects?**

Vocabulary School subjects

Art Computer studies English Geography History Maths Music P.E. Science

3 **Which school subjects need these things?**

1 paints, scissors – *Art*
2 map
3 dictionary
4 tracksuit, trainers
5 calculator, ruler
6 piano, guitar

Grammar *be going to*

+	–
I'm going to study.	I'm not going to study.
You/We/They're going to study.	You/We/They aren't going to study.
He/She/It's going to study.	He/She/It isn't going to study.
?	**Short answers**
Am I going to study?	Yes, I am. / No, I'm not.
Are you/we/they going to study?	Yes, you/we/they are. No, you/we/they aren't.
Is he/she/it going to study?	Yes, he/she/it is. No, he/she/it isn't.

4 **Complete the sentences with the correct form of *be going to*. Then guess who's talking.**

1 My parents and I *are going to go* (go) shopping for a laptop! *Poppy*
2 I ____________ (have) chicken and some salad for lunch, not pizza.
3 Gran, ______ you ____________ (help) me study for the Geography test?
4 ______ my brother ____________ (get up) late again? I ____________ (not wait) for him.
5 ______ we ____________ (buy) a laptop case too?

5 1.7 **Listen and repeat. Does your school have all of these places?**

Vocabulary Places in a school

canteen classroom computer room gym hall library playground staff room

6 1.8 **Where are the people? Listen and write the places.**

1 *in the playground*

Fun Spot

7 **Choose a place. Play *What are you going to do there?***

A: *I'm going to go to the canteen.*
B: *Are you going to have lunch there?*
A: *No, I'm not. I'm going to read a book.*

Meet Doctor Q and his friends

This is Doctor Q. He's a brilliant scientist and inventor. Doctor Q is very interested in art and he loves painting. This is why he is very excited about his new invention.

Pi, the parrot, is Doctor Q's best friend. He loves playing video games on Doctor Q's lab computer. Doctor Q hates it!

Rob and Millie are Doctor Q's assistants. They are very intelligent and friendly robots. They work with Doctor Q in the lab and they are very helpful at home.

Rob and Millie are very kind. Rob is bad at cooking and Millie doesn't like cleaning, so Rob helps Millie with the cleaning and she helps him with the cooking.

1 1.9 **Listen and read. Circle T (true) or F (false).**

1 Doctor Q is a very good scientist. (T) / F
2 Pi doesn't like computer games. T / F
3 Rob is a brilliant chef. T / F
4 Millie likes helping Rob. T / F

2 1.10 **Listen and repeat. Circle the feelings.**

Vocabulary Adjectives

angry bored friendly funny happy
helpful intelligent kind sad tired

3 Look at the cartoon. How do they feel? Use the adjectives in the Vocabulary box.

Picture 1: Pi is *bored* .
Picture 2: Doctor Q is ________ .
Picture 3: Rob is ________ . Millie is ________ .
Picture 4: Rob and Millie are ________ .

4 In pairs, use the remaining adjectives to describe the other cartoon characters.

A: *Doctor Q is intelligent.*
B: *I think he's funny too.*

5 1.11 **Listen and repeat. Which of the words are positive?**

Vocabulary Adjectives with prepositions

bad at good at excited about worried about
interested in scared of

6 1.12 **What does Doctor Q say? Match 1–6 to a–f. Then listen and check.**

1 [e] I'm bad
2 [ ] I'm excited
3 [ ] I'm worried
4 [ ] I'm good
5 [ ] I'm scared
6 [ ] I'm interested

a about my new invention. It's fantastic!
b of spiders.
c about Pi. I can't find him anywhere.
d in science.
e at skiing. I often fall.
f at inventing things!

7 Write a short presentation about yourself. Use the words in the Vocabulary boxes. Share in pairs.

I feel happy when …
I'm interested in …

I can talk about food and its quantity. **Is there any milk?** 0.5

In the kitchen

Doctor Q and Millie love cooking.

Dr Q: Can I have the flour, please Millie?
Millie: Yes, of course. What are we going to make?
Dr Q: We're going to make …

1 1.13 **Look at the picture. Listen and read. What do you think Doctor Q and Millie are going to make? Go to page 106 and check.**

Grammar Countable and uncountable nouns, *some* and *any*

Countable nouns	Uncountable nouns
an apple	sugar
There **are some** apples.	There **is some** sugar.
There **aren't any** apples.	There **isn't any** sugar.
Are there **any** apples?	**Is** there **any** sugar?
How many apples **are** there?	**How much** sugar **is** there?
There **are ten** apples.	There **are two packets of** sugar.

2 1.14 **Listen and repeat. In your notebook, make two lists: countable and uncountable nouns.**

Vocabulary Food and drink

apple biscuit bread butter carrot
cereal chocolate cucumber egg
flour juice orange rice strawberry
sugar tuna water yoghurt

Countable: *apple, biscuit, …*
Uncountable: *bread, butter, …*

3 Look at the picture and complete the sentences with the correct form of the verb *to be* and *some* or *any*.

1 There *are* *some* apples.
2 There ______ ______ coffee.
3 There ______ ______ biscuits.
4 There ______ ______ milk.
5 There ______ ______ eggs.
6 There ______ ______ cucumbers.

4 1.15 **Listen and repeat. Label the containers in Doctor Q's kitchen.**

Vocabulary Containers

a bar of chocolate a bottle of water
a can of tuna a carton of milk
a jar of jam a packet of flour

a *a bottle of water* d ______
b ______ e ______
c ______ f ______

5 1.16 **Complete the questions. Look at the picture and answer. Then listen and check.**

1 How *many* apples ______ there?
2 How ______ tuna ______ there?
3 How ______ eggs ______ there?
4 How ______ flour ______ there?
5 How ______ water ______ there?
6 How ______ chocolate ______ there?

A: *How many apples are there?*
B: *There are five apples.*

Fun Spot

6 Work in pairs. Student A: Make a list of ten food and drink items. Student B: Find out what is on A's list. Hurry up! You have only two minutes! Then swap roles.

B: *Is there any jam?*
B: *Are there any apples?*
B: *How many apples are there?*

A: *No, there isn't any jam.*
A: *Yes, there are some apples.*
A: *Six.*

1 Life at home

Vocabulary I can talk about household chores.

In this unit

Vocabulary
- Household chores
- Personality adjectives

Grammar
- Present Continuous
- Stative verbs
- Present Simple and Present Continuous

2-3

1.2 Grammar video

4

1.2 Grammar animation

5

1.3 Grammar animation

6

1.4 Communication video

7

BBC Culture video

I know that!

1 How often do you do these things: usually, sometimes or never?

make breakfast cook lunch or dinner
make your bed wash the dishes tidy your room
wash your clothes look after your brother/sister

1

2

3

4

What a chore!

Vote for the best and the worst household chores!

5

6

7

2 1.17 **Listen and read. Which of these activities can you see in the photos on page 10?**

Vocabulary Household chores

clear the table empty the dishwasher feed the dog
hang out the washing iron your T-shirt
load the dishwasher load the washing machine
make your bed put away your clothes
set the table take out the rubbish
vacuum your room water the plants

3 Label the pictures with the household chores in the Vocabulary box.

1 *clear the table*

2 ______

3 ______

4 ______

5 ______

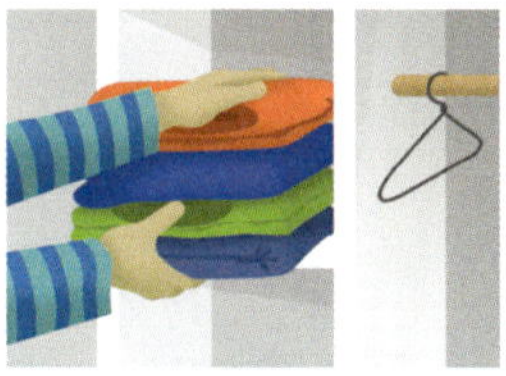

6 ______

4 Work in pairs. Who usually does the chores in Exercise 3 in your family? Compare with a partner.

My sister usually clears the table.

5 1.18 **Listen to the dialogues. What do you think the people say? Match 1–5 to a–e.**

1 [d] Angie's mum
2 [ ] Ben's dad
3 [ ] Jayne's mum
4 [ ] Jimmy's mum
5 [ ] Sarah's dad

a You can set the table.
b Feed the cat, please.
c Can you take out the rubbish, please?
d Put away your clothes!
e Load the washing machine for me.

6 1.19 **Now listen to the complete dialogues and check your answers to Exercise 5.**

7 Act out the dialogues in pairs.

1 The dogs are very hungry!
A: *The dogs are very hungry!*
B: *No problem. I can feed them.*
2 There are lots of dirty clothes.
3 The bin in the kitchen is full.
4 The carpet in the living room is dirty.
5 The dishes in the dishwasher are clean.
6 Dinner's ready!
7 Look at the poor plants!

8 Exam Spot Complete the blog post with the words in the box. There are two extra words.

doing feeding ironing loading
making putting ~~setting~~
taking vacuuming watering

Which chores do you like? Which ones do you hate?

Jason

I don't like [1]*setting* the table or clearing it after meals, and I don't like [2]______ and emptying the dishwasher. It's boring! I hate [3]______ out the rubbish! That's a smelly chore! I like [4]______ the carpet in my bedroom, [5]______ away my clothes and [6]______ my bed because I like having a tidy bedroom. I like [7]______ the plants too. And I love [8]______ my dogs, Rusty and Mustard. They're my best friends.

I remember that!

9 Complete the table below with household chores.

I like	I hate
watering the plants	*loading the dishwasher*

Compare your answers in pairs. Discuss the reasons for your choices.

boring / fun difficult / easy
smelly / smell(s) nice

A: *I hate loading the dishwasher.*
B: *Why?*
A: *Because it's boring!*

1.2 **Grammar** I can use the Present Continuous.

I'm vacuuming

It's Saturday morning. George and Harry are playing a computer game. Their cousin, Emma, is at school.

1

Harry: I love this game!
George: Emma's calling.
Emma: Hi, guys!
George: Hi, Emma! What's up?
Emma: I'm calling because I need your help.
George: What kind of help?
Emma: I'm making decorations for the school fair. Look!
Harry: Nice! I like them!
Emma: Thanks, but I can't finish them on my own. It's a lot of work.
George: Can't your classmates help you?
Emma: Not really. They're all very busy. Please?

2

George: Well … erm … I don't know … I'm rather busy too. I'm … I'm vacuuming right now.
Emma: Nice try! I can see the game controller! What about you, Harry? Are you vacuuming too?
Harry: No, I'm not. I've got … tennis practice. Bye!
George: Sorry, Emma!
Emma: Yeah, right!

A little later …

3

George: It's a text from Emma.
Harry: What is she saying?

1 2 1.20 **Watch or listen and read. Why is Emma calling George and Harry?**

2 Complete the sentences.

1 The boys aren't *at school* today because it's Saturday.
2 Emma's making __________ for the school fair.
3 All of Emma's __________ are very busy at the moment.
4 George says he's busy because he wants to stay at home and play the __________ .
5 Harry hasn't really got __________ .

3 1.21 **Listen and repeat. Find these expressions in the story.**

Say it!

Not really. Nice try! Yeah, right!

4 **Guess!** **What's Emma saying in her text? Have a class vote.**

5 3 1.22 **Now watch or listen and check.**

Grammar Present Continuous

+	–
I'm playing.	I'm not playing.
He/She/It's playing.	He/She/It isn't playing.
You/We/They're playing.	You/We/They aren't playing.
?	**Short answers**
Am I playing?	Yes, I am. / No, I'm not.
Is he/she/it playing?	Yes, he/she/it is. No, he/she/it isn't.
Are you/we/they playing?	Yes, you/we/they are. No, you/we/they aren't.

What are they doing? Why is she calling?

4 Get Grammar!

6 It's Saturday afternoon. Complete the sentences with the Present Continuous form of the verb.

1 George and Harry *are doing* (do) their chores. They ________ (not play) a computer game.
2 Emma ________ (not make) decorations for the school fair. She ________ (put) away the clean clothes.
3 The boys' mum and dad ________ (have) a cup of coffee. They ________ (not watch) TV.
4 Poppy and her parents ________ (not tidy) the house. They ________ (do) the shopping.

7 It's Saturday evening now. Complete the telephone conversation. Write questions and short answers.

Emma: Hi, Gran. [1]*Are you calling* (you / call) from home?
Gran: No, [2]________ . I'm at a café with a friend. [3]________ (you / hang out) with Poppy?
Emma: Yes, [4]________ . We're cooking spaghetti at her place.
Gran: Great. [5]________ (Poppy's mum / help) you?
Emma: No, [6]________ . She's working in the garden.

Grammar Stative verbs

We don't usually use the Present Continuous with these verbs: like, love, hate, know, need, understand, want.

I want a sandwich. ✔ NOT ~~I'm wanting a sandwich.~~ ✗

8 Which stative verbs can you find in the story on page 12?

9 Complete the text messages with the Present Continuous or the Present Simple form of the verbs in the box.

do ~~study~~ love need watch like want

Hi, [1]*are* you *studying* ?
No, I'm not. I [2]________ a film.
[3]________ you ________ it?
No, I don't. It's silly.

[4]________ you ________ the shopping?
Yes, I am.
Please, buy some chocolate, I [5]________ to make a cake.
Sure. I [6]________ your cakes! [7]________ you ________ anything else?
Yes, some orange juice, please.

10 Exam Spot Work in pairs.
Student A: Go to page 106.
Student B: Go to page 112.

1.3 Grammar

I can use the Present Simple and the Present Continuous.

Doctor Q — Doctor Q's day off

1 Look at the cartoon. What's in Doctor Q's newest painting?

2 1.23 Listen and read. Does Doctor Q work a lot?

3 Read the sentences. Circle the correct answer.

1 Pi thinks Doctor Q *often has* / *doesn't have* fun.
2 *Millie* / *Rob* is looking for Doctor Q.
3 Rob *knows* / *doesn't know* where Doctor Q is.
4 Doctor Q usually dances *once a year* / *every week*.
5 Doctor Q *doesn't usually skateboard* / *often skateboards*.

Grammar Present Simple and Present Continuous

Present Simple	Present Continuous
I often **watch** TV.	I'**m watching** TV right now.
Doctor Q **works** every day.	Doctor Q **is working** at the moment.
Time expressions	
every day, every week *on Fridays, on weekdays* *at the weekend* *always, never, usually, often, sometimes*	*now* *right now* *at the moment* *today*

5 Get Grammar!

4 Read the sentences from the cartoon. Decide and write R (regularly) or N (now).

1 [N] I'm working!
2 [ ] You work every day!
3 [ ] He usually starts at 9 a.m.
4 [ ] They're playing the drums!
5 [ ] He only dances on his birthday.
6 [ ] I'm going to bed.

5 Read the sentences and circle the correct answer.

1 Rob and Millie *clean* / *are cleaning* the lab on Mondays. Right now, Rob *vacuums* / *is vacuuming* the floor and Millie *tidies* / *is tidying* Doctor Q's desk.

2 Doctor Q *sleeps* / *is sleeping* at the moment. He usually *gets up* / *is getting up* at 8 a.m.

3 Doctor Q usually *listens* / *is listening* to classical music. He *downloads* / *is downloading* his favourite opera at the moment.

4 Doctor Q and Pi often *watch* / *are watching* a DVD in the evenings. They *watch* / *are watching* a comedy right now.

6 1.24 Listen to the dialogues. Complete the sentences with the words in the brackets in the correct form.

1 Lucy *writes her blog* every day, but right now she ____________ . (write her blog, chat online)
2 Lucy usually ____________ , but today she ____________ . (wear jeans, wear a dress)
3 Lucy always ____________ on Mondays, but tonight she ____________ . (stay at home, have dinner at a restaurant)

7 In pairs, ask and answer questions about Lucy in Exercise 6.

A: *What does Lucy do every day?*
B: *She writes her blog.*
A: *What is she doing right now?*
B: *She's chatting …*

Fun Spot

8 Today is 'Be Different Day'! What are you doing to make it different? Complete the table and tell your friends.

	usually	today
morning	*have toast*	*have pancakes*
afternoon		
evening		

It's seven o'clock in the morning. I usually have toast for breakfast, but right now I'm having pancakes!

1.4 Communication I can ask for help and offer help.

Do you need any help?

Gran: Emma, I need some help, please.
Emma: No problem, Gran. Just coming!
Gran: Can you help me with the sofa, please? I'd like to move it.
Emma: Yes, of course but … why?
Gran: This room's boring. Let's change things a little.

Fifteen minutes later …
Emma: Do you need any help with the lamp?
Gran: No, that's fine, thank you …
Emma: OK, then. I'm going to Poppy's.
Gran: … but can you move the coffee table, please? I don't think it looks good here.
Emma: OK.

Twenty minutes later …
Gran: I think the living room looks perfect now.
Emma: Gran, it looks the same as it was before!
Gran: What?

1 6 **1.25 Watch or listen and read. Then answer the questions.**

1 Does Gran like the room after the changes?
2 Is the living room different in the end?

2 **1.26 Listen and repeat.**

> **Communication**
> **Asking for and offering help**
>
> **Asking for help**
> Can you help me *with the sofa*, please?
> Can you *move the coffee table*, please?
> **Reacting**
> No problem. / Yes, of course.
> I'm sorry, I can't. I'm *busy right now*.
>
> **Offering help**
> Can I help you *with the lamp*?
> Do you need any help *with the lamp*?
> **Reacting**
> Yes, please. / No, that's fine, thank you.

3 **1.27 Complete the dialogues with one word in each gap. Then listen and check.**

1 **Mum:** Max! Can you [1]*help* me with the housework?
Max: No [2]________, Mum.
Mum: Can you load the dishwasher, [3]________ ?
Max: Yes, of [4]________ !

2 **Max:** Do you need any help [5]________ the cooking?
Mum: Yes, please. [6]________ you wash the tomatoes?

3 **Dad:** Max, can you download this song for me?
Max: I'm [7]________ , Dad, I [8]________ . I'm cooking right now!

4 Work in pairs. Take turns to ask for and offer help with:

1 the housework (load the washing machine, set the table).
A: *Can you help me with the housework?*
B: *No problem.*
A: *Can you … ?*
2 the shopping (go to the supermarket, put the shopping away).
A: *Do you need any help with the shopping?*
B: *Yes, please. Can you … ?*
3 the cooking (bring the ingredients to the table, wash the potatoes).
4 the plants (take them to the garden, water them).

1 Look at the photos. What do you think the children are doing?

2 1.28 Read and listen to the text. Match photos A–C to paragraphs 1–3.

3 **Exam Spot** Choose the best title for the text.

a Only children – how happy are they?
b Which is better – a big or a small family?
c Brothers and sisters – love them or hate them?

4 Read the text again. Answer the questions. Write B (Ben), L (Lizzie) or R (Robbie). Who:

1 [L] sometimes argues with his/her brothers/sisters?
2 [ ] has got a pet?
3 [ ] often does a brother's/sister's chores?
4 [ ] likes being on his/her own?
5 [ ] isn't worried about what his/her brothers/sisters say?
6 [ ] has got only one brother?

5 1.29 Listen and repeat. Find the words in the text.

Vocabulary Personality adjectives

bossy easy-going loud messy organised patient quiet tidy

6 Circle the correct answer.

Wendy, 14

- Dad is a [1] (quiet) / *bossy* man. He doesn't talk a lot, but he always listens to us.
- My mum's [2] *loud / easy-going*. She doesn't get angry when our bedrooms are untidy.
- My big twin sisters are [3] *organised / loud*! They always shout when they argue!
- My brother is [4] *messy / patient*. He never puts his clothes away.
- I'm [5] *quiet / tidy*. I like putting things in the right place.
- Gran plans everything and she knows where everything is. She's [6] *easy-going / organised*.

7 What are the members of your family like? Ask and answer in pairs.

A: *What's your mum like?*
B: *She's organised, but she isn't patient. She hates waiting.*

A

B

C

Find out what our readers wrote about their families.

1 [ ] **Ben, 14**

Living with my sister is so difficult! She's very messy. She's six, so her only chores are putting her toys away and feeding our cat, Mr Paws. Her toys are always on the floor and Mr Paws' bowl is usually empty! I'm tidy and organised, so I often do her chores in the end. I love her, but I think I'm too patient with her!

2 [ ] **Lizzie, 13**

I'm the only girl in the family. My brothers say I'm too loud and the neighbours can hear me when I talk, but that's not true. We sometimes argue about what to watch on TV. All brothers and sisters argue sometimes! My brothers usually win and I watch the things they like, even the football. But I'm easy-going and I don't get upset easily.

3 [ ] **Robbie, 12**

I'm very quiet and I like spending time on my own. I like reading or playing video games in my room. My brother is very different from me. He can't spend one minute on his own! He is also very bossy. He always tells me what to do! Sometimes I think my best friend, Chris, is lucky – he is an only child!

Write to us and tell us about your family!

1.6 Listening and Writing

I can understand a radio programme.
I can write a simple essay.

1 **I know that!** **Look at the words in the box. Circle the activities you do with your family. Add as many as you can.**

have breakfast go to school
chat online feed the dog watch TV
go to the cinema play football
tidy my room ride my bike

2 **1.30 Where are Andy and his family going? Listen and tick (✔) the correct picture. Are the other two places important for Andy's family?**

A ☐

B ☐

C ☐

3 **1.30 Listen again. Circle T (true) or F (false).**

1 It's Saturday afternoon. T / F
2 Andy and his family always spend time together on Sundays. T / F
3 Andy's mum is driving the car. T / F
4 Andy's mum gives Sue a sandwich. T / F
5 Andy helps his sisters with their homework. T / F

4 **Read Hattie's essay. What activities does she do with her family?**

Family time

by Hattie Jones

1 In my family, we don't do a lot of things together on weekdays because we're very busy. We don't usually have dinner as a family, but we sometimes watch TV together. We love programmes about animals!

2 On Saturdays, I do my chores. I put away my clothes and I vacuum my room. Then I meet my friends. I come back home at 7.30 p.m. because we always have a family dinner in the evening. On Sundays, we often visit my grandparents. They don't live near, so Mum drives us to their house. We have a lot of fun together.

5 **Read the Writing box. Then underline sentences with *and*, *but*, *because* and *so* in Hattie's essay.**

Writing *and, but, because, so*

Dad sets the table for dinner ***and*** *Hattie helps him.*
I love swimming, ***but*** *I can't go to the pool every day.*
I go to bed early on weekdays ***because*** *I have school in the morning.*
Mum opens her shop at 8.30 a.m., ***so*** *she leaves home at 7.45 a.m.*

6 **Writing Time** **Write an essay about the activities you do with your family.**

Find ideas
Think about the activities you do with your family on weekdays and at the weekend. Make notes.

Draft
Write two paragraphs about your family.
In my family, we do/don't do a lot of things together on weekdays.
We always/usually/often/sometimes/never …
On Saturdays, I/we/my family …
On Sundays, …

Check and write
Check the use of *and*, *but*, *because* and *so* and write the final version of your essay.

Vocabulary

1 Complete the texts with the words in the box.

clear feed iron load make put ~~set~~ hang out vacuum water

Everyone does chores in our house. I [1]*set* the table for lunch. Then I [2]________ the table after lunch. I take the dirty dishes to the kitchen and [3]________ the dishwasher.

I look after our clothes. I [4]________ the washing, [5]________ the clothes and [6]________ them away. I [7]________ the plants too.

I [8]________ the floor and the carpets and [9]________ my bed. I also [10]________ the dog.

2 Read and write the words.

1 I don't mind waiting for people. **p***atient*
2 I don't make a noise and I don't talk a lot. **q**________
3 I like telling people what to do. **b**________
4 I never tidy my room. **m**________
5 I put my things in the right place and I plan everything. **o**________
6 I'm not often angry or worried. **e**________

Grammar

3 Complete the dialogue with the correct forms of the Present Continuous.

George: Hi, Mum. What [1]*are you doing* (you / do)?
Mum: I [2]____________ (make) dinner at the moment.
George: I'm at David's. We [3]____________ (watch) the football. Is Harry there?
Mum: Yes, he is. He [4]____________ (help) Dad in the garden. They [5]____________ (water) the plants.
George: Can I speak to him? He [6]____________ (not answer) his mobile.
Mum: Yes, of course. Harry! HARRY! [7]____________ (you / come)?

4 Complete the text with the correct form of the verbs in the box.

know love need ~~want~~ not like

Hi, Mum. I [1]*want* to buy new jeans. The black jeans are only £10, but I [2]________ them. I [3]________ the blue jeans. They're cool but they're expensive and I [4]________ some money now. I [5]________ it's not pocket money time, but …

5 Circle the correct answer.

Andy's parents are at work. They always [1]*open / are opening* their pet shop early on Saturday because people often [2]*buy / are buying* pet food at the weekend. At the moment they [3]*serve / are serving* customers. There are also some children in the shop. They [4]*look / are looking* at the tropical fish. Children often [5]*come / are coming* to the shop but they [6]*don't often buy / aren't often buying* anything.

Pronunciation

6 1.31 Listen and repeat: /ʃ/.

Your special T-shirt's
in the washing machine.
Be patient and wait
till it is fresh and clean.

Communication

7 1.32 In your notebook, write questions. Listen and check. Then write the replies.

1 you housework help Do with need the any ? ✔
A: *Do you need any help with the housework?*
B: *Yes, please.*
2 dishwasher, you the load Can please ? ✘
3 you away please put Can these clothes, ? ✔
4 with help Can the I you cooking ? ✘

Check yourself!

- I can talk about household chores. ☐
- I can use the Present Simple and the Present Continuous. ☐
- I can ask for help and offer help. ☐

Get Culture!

Unusual places to live

Izzie's most unusual places

Hi, I'm Izzie and this is my blog about the most unusual places in the world. Today I'm writing about Australia!

Australia is a continent and it's also an English-speaking country. Its capital is Canberra and three of its largest cities are Sydney, Melbourne and Brisbane. Australia is the sixth largest country in the world, but only about twenty-five million people live there. Desert covers most of the land, so about eighty percent of the people live on the coast. The climate is better there. But some people live in unusual places. One of them is a small town called Coober Pedy.

Coober Pedy is in the South Australian desert. On summer days, it can be as hot as 47ºC! For this reason, more than half the people live under the ground. The temperature is always comfortable there. Underground homes have kitchens, bathrooms, bedrooms and living rooms. Everyday life in Coober Pedy is not very different from any other town. People go to work or school, do their household chores, watch TV and spend time with friends and family.

Coober Pedy has lots of visitors every year. People come to stay in the underground hotels. There are also underground shops, cafés and museums. On summer nights, when it isn't too hot, people can go above the ground and play golf in the world's only golf course without grass. It's not easy to lose golf balls because they are glow-in-the-dark!

1 **Read the text about Australia quickly. What do these numbers refer to?**

6 25 80 47

2 **1.33 Listen and read. Circle the correct words.**

1 The capital city of Australia is *Sydney / Canberra*.
2 There *are big / aren't any* deserts in Australia.
3 Coober Pedy is *on the coast / in the desert*.
4 *All / Some* of the people in Coober Pedy live under the ground.
5 *Not many / A lot of* people go to see Coober Pedy every year.
6 There *are / aren't any* underground hotels in Coober Pedy.

3 **1.34 Listen to two people talking about cities in Australia. Find the cities on the map in Izzie's blog. Then complete the factfiles.**

Darwin

- In the 1 *rainy* season, there are storms and it's very hot.
- Swimming in the sea is dangerous because there are 2 ________ in the water.
- You can buy 3 ________ from all over the world at the Mindil Beach Sunset Market.

Sydney

- Sydney has more than 4 ________ beaches.
- Bondi Beach is the most 5 ________ beach.
- Australians love doing 6 ________ .
- Sydney has a lot of parks and a 7 ________ .

4 **Which place in Australia would you most like to visit? Give your reasons.**

The Arctic

A ▶ 7 **Watch the video and answer the presenter's question. How do people get around in the Arctic in winter?**

B ▶ 7 **Watch the video again. Circle T (true) or F (false).**

1 The Canadian flag is red and yellow. **T / F**
2 Vancouver is a city in Canada. **T / F**
3 Fifty percent of Canada is in the Arctic. **T / F**
4 People sometimes build igloos in the Arctic. **T / F**
5 Winter in the Arctic can last from October to March. **T / F**
6 In the summer, there are days when it doesn't get light. **T / F**

C **Imagine you are living in the Arctic. It's late November. What can you do at the weekend? Discuss your answers as a class.**

PROJECT

- **Work in groups. Design a town or a city which is in a very unusual place. Think of a name and location. Use these words or your own ideas.**

in a rain forest　on a different planet
on top of a mountain　under the sea

- **Write a tourist guide about your town/city for a travel magazine. Use these questions to help you.**

  Where is the town/city?
  What can you see there? (e.g. buildings, parks, hotels, museums, zoos)
  What kind of homes do people have?
  What can you do there?

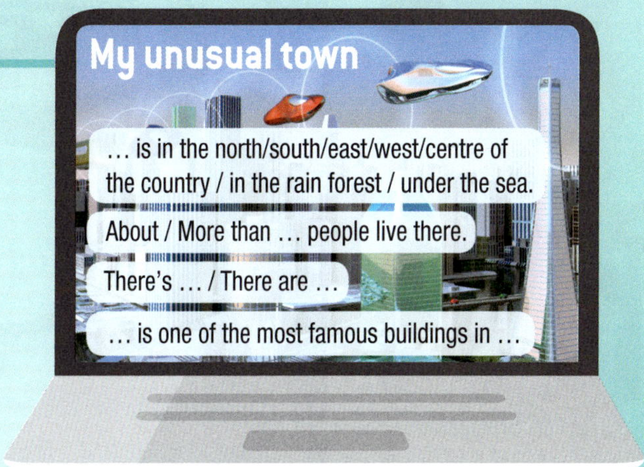

- **Find photos or draw some pictures. Put the text and pictures together.**
- **Present your guide to the class. Vote for the most unusual town or city.**

2 Shopping

Vocabulary I can talk about shopping.

In this unit

Vocabulary
- Shopping
- Shops

Grammar
- Comparative and superlative adjectives
- *too … , not … enough, (not) as … as*

▶ 8-9

2.2 Grammar video

▶ 10

2.2 Grammar animation

▶ 11

2.3 Grammar animation

▶ 12

2.4 Communication video

I know that!

1 Do you prefer shopping at a supermarket or in a small shop? Why? Use the words below to explain.

boring / exciting busy / empty cheap / expensive quick / slow small / big

2 1.35 **Listen and repeat. Look at the picture on page 22 and answer the questions below the Vocabulary box.**

Vocabulary Shopping

Nouns

cashier shopping bag shopping basket shopping list shoping trolley special offer

Phrases

carry the shopping check the price get a receipt get your change pay by card pay for the shopping pay in cash stand in a queue

Who is:

a holding a shopping list?
b paying for the shopping?
c standing in a queue?

3 **Look at the picture again. How many can you find?**

a shopping trolleys [5]
b shopping baskets [ ]
c shopping bags [ ]
d cashiers [ ]
e queues [ ]
f special offers [ ]

4 **Look at the photos and complete the expressions.**

1 pay in *cash*

2 get your ______

3 get a ______

4 check the ______

5 pay by ______

6 carry the ______

5 **Exam Spot** **Match the words in the box to definitions 1–6. There are two extra words.**

card cashier price ~~shopping bag~~ shopping basket shopping list shopping trolley special offer

1 You use it to carry your shopping home. *shopping bag*
2 This person takes your money and gives you change. ______
3 You write this to remember the things you want to buy. ______
4 It's big, it's got four wheels and you push it around the supermarket. ______
5 You put things in this at the supermarket. You don't push it. You carry it, but you don't take it home. ______
6 When something is cheaper than it usually is. ______

6 1.36 **What do you do when you go shopping? Put the sentences in the correct order. Then listen and check.**

a [1] Take a basket.
b [ ] Carry the shopping to the car.
c [ ] Put your shopping in the basket.
d [ ] Get your change and your receipt.
e [ ] Pay for the shopping in cash.
f [ ] Stand in a queue.
g [8] Go home and put the shopping away.
h [ ] Check the price.

7 1.37 **Listen and match dialogues 1–5 to sentences a–h in Exercise 6. There are three extra sentences.**

1 [f] 2 [ ] 3 [ ] 4 [ ] 5 [ ]

I remember that!

8 **Work in pairs. Write three true and three false sentences about the picture on page 22. Use the words in the Vocabulary box.**

The woman's shopping list is very long.

9 **Read your sentences to the class. Your classmates say which sentences are true.**

I can use comparative and superlative adjectives.

The green bag is the best

George and Harry's mum and Gran Bertie are going out.

1

Gran: Oh, no! There's a hole in my bag!
Mum: Mum, this bag is older than I am! I think you need a new one.
Gran: You're right, but you know I hate shopping, dear! Let's go.
Mum: Bye, boys!
Harry: Bye!
George: Have fun!

2

George: Let's buy Gran a new bag for her birthday!
Harry: Good idea! Women's bags … Here we are!
George: How about the yellow one?
Harry: It doesn't look big. Gran likes big bags. And it's £100.
George: I like the red bag too. It's cheaper and bigger than the yellow one.
Harry: It's £80! We've only got £50.
George: Hmm … Let's try another site.
Harry: The green one is the best. It's the most stylish and the cheapest too. Only £25!
George: I agree.

A few days later …

3

Mum: I think it's for you, boys.
Harry: Thanks, Mum. Gran's present! Let's see … I don't believe it!

1 8 1.38 Watch or listen and read. Why do the boys want to buy Gran a new bag?

2 Match photos A–C to sentences 1–3. Which bag do the boys choose?

A 

B 

C 

1 ☐ It's £25. 2 ☐ It's £100. 3 ☐ It's £80.

3 1.39 Listen and repeat. Find these expressions in the story.

Say it!

Have fun! Here we are!
I don't believe it!

4 Guess! Why is Harry surprised? Make a guess.

5 9 1.40 Now watch or listen and check.

Grammar
Comparative and superlative adjectives

Adjective	Comparative	Superlative
Short adjectives		
small	smaller	the smallest
nice	nicer	the nicest
big	bigger	the biggest
busy	busier	the busiest
Long adjectives		
boring	more boring	the most boring
expensive	more expensive	the most expensive
Irregular adjectives		
good	better	the best
bad	worse	the worst

The blue bag is **bigger than** the brown bag.
He's a **better** student **than** his brother.
This is **the most expensive** T-shirt in the shop.

▶ 10 Get Grammar!

6 **Complete the sentences about Harry and George with the comparative form of the adjectives.**

1 young
2 sporty
3 good at tennis
4 fast runner

Harry is [1] *younger* than George. He's [2] ________ than his brother. He's [3] ________ at tennis and he's also a [4] ________ runner than George.

5 funny
6 stylish
7 organised
8 good dancer

George is [5] ________ than Harry. His clothes are [6] ________ than his brother's. He's also [7] ________ and he's a [8] ________ dancer than Harry.

7 **Complete George's opinions with the superlative form of the adjectives in brackets.**

1 I am *the funniest* (funny) person I know!
2 I think Emma is ________ (intelligent) student in her class.
3 Mum is ________ (good) cook in the world!
4 *The Long Way* is ________ (interesting) film on TV tonight.
5 I can't watch Dad in this video! He's ________ (bad) dancer in the family!
6 I hate vacuuming. It's ________ (boring) thing in the world!

8 🔊 1.41 **Complete the text with a comparative form and *than* or a superlative form of the adjectives in the box. Then listen and check.**

big fast dangerous ~~expensive~~ exciting

Say what you think!

Theatre and cinema

Lucas, 14
Theatre tickets are [1] *more expensive than* cinema tickets, but I love seeing my favourite actors in real life!

Jane, 13
For me, the cinema is [2] ________ the theatre. I love big screens. The cinema in the shopping centre near my house has [3] ________ screen in the UK!

Bikes and motorbikes

Laura, 14
I've got a bike. They are not [4] ________ way to travel, but they are good for our health.

Paul, 15
People say that motorbikes are [5] ________ bikes because they go very fast. I don't agree. If the motorcyclist is careful, motorbikes are safe.

Doctor Q The shopping

1

Dear Millie and Rob,
Please do some shopping for me.
xxx
Cornelius Q

Here's the list:

good shampoo
some tasty apples
some interesting books
today's newspaper
fresh bread

2

Millie: Hello, have you got good shampoo?
Chemist: Good shampoo? *Nice Hair* is very good and it's on special offer today. It's not as expensive as *Great Hair*.
Millie: Good! How many bottles do we need?
Rob: The list doesn't say. Erm … let's take ten bottles.

3

Rob: 'Tasty apples' … The list isn't clear enough. Which apples does Doctor Q like? I think these are too small. These are too big and these … aren't red enough.
Millie: I think they all look tasty. Let's buy all of them.

4

Millie: 'Interesting books' … I think these science-fiction books are as interesting as those science books. I can't choose!
Rob: Let's buy them all. Doctor Q likes reading.

Two hours later …

5

Rob: Here's your shopping, Doctor Q.
Millie: And here are your receipts.
Dr Q: Oh …
Pi: Doctor Q? What's wrong?

1 Look at picture 1. What's Doctor Q's first name?

2 1.42 Read and listen. Circle T (true) or F (false).

1 The chemist hasn't got good shampoo. T / F
2 Millie and Rob buy the shampoo on special offer. T / F
3 There are different types of apples at the shop. T / F
4 Rob doesn't want to buy any books. T / F
5 Doctor Q isn't shocked when he sees the receipts. T / F

Grammar
too, not … enough, (not) as … as

▶ 11 **Get Grammar!**

too + adjective
These apples are too small.
not + adjective + enough
This list isn't (is not) clear enough.
(not) as + adjective + as
These books are as interesting as those books.
Nice Hair isn't (is not) as expensive as *Great Hair*.

3 🔊 1.43 **Complete the dialogues with *too* or *not … enough* and the adjectives in the box. Then listen and check.**

~~big~~ boring fast quiet warm

1 **Pi:** My new hat is too small!
Millie: Yes, you're right. It's *not big enough* .
2 **Rob:** This science book is __________ !
Dr Q: I agree. It's not interesting enough.
3 **Dr Q:** The water is too cold.
Pi: Yes, it's __________ .
4 **Pi:** This music is __________ .
Dr Q: Yes, it's not loud enough.
5 **Pi:** This tablet is too slow!
Rob: You're right. It's __________ .

4 **Compare Rob and Millie. Write sentences with *as … as* or *not as … as*.**

1 Rob is older than Millie. Millie …
Millie isn't as old as Rob.
2 Rob and Millie are friendly. Millie …
Millie is as friendly as Rob.
3 Millie is stronger than Rob. Rob …
4 Rob is faster than Millie. Millie …
5 Rob and Millie are intelligent. Rob …
6 Millie and Rob are 1.60 metres tall. Millie …

5 🔊 1.44 **Listen and repeat. Which shops can you see in the cartoon?**

Vocabulary Shops

baker's bookshop chemist's clothes shop
department store greengrocer's
newsagent's shoe shop sports shop

6 **Where can you buy these things? Write the shops. Then act out dialogues in pairs.**

1 a sofa, a skirt and a cup – *department store*
A: *Where can you buy a sofa, a skirt and a cup?*
B: *At a department store.*
2 tennis balls and trainers
3 vitamins and thermometer
4 bread and cakes
5 jeans and dresses
6 newspapers and magazines
7 fruit and vegetables
8 boots and shoes
9 school books and comic books

7 **Write three sentences about the shops in your area. Use *too …* , *not … enough*, and *(not) as … as*.**

bad boring busy cheap clean dirty exciting expensive friendly good long modern new old quiet short

The department store in our town isn't as big as the department stores in London.
The queues at the supermarket are too long.

Can I try it on?

Assistant: Can I help you?
Poppy: No, thanks. We're just looking.
Emma: Poppy, how about this jacket?
Poppy: I like it, but I'm not sure about the colour … Excuse me? Do you have this in grey?
Assistant: Yes, we do. What size are you?
Poppy: 8.
Assistant: Here you are. Size 8.
Poppy: Thank you.
Emma: I like this T-shirt. Can I try it on?
Assistant: Yes, of course. The changing rooms are over there.

Emma: The jacket looks fantastic!
Poppy: And I love your T-shirt! I want one too!
Emma: Here's an idea: You can borrow my T-shirt …
Poppy: … and you can borrow my jacket!
Emma: We're so clever!

1 12 1.45 **Watch or listen and read. What do Emma and Poppy want to buy at the shop?**

2 1.46 **Listen and repeat.**

Communication Shopping for clothes

Shop assistant

Can I help you?
What size are you?
Yes, we do. Here you are. / Sorry, we don't.
The changing rooms are over there.

Customer

I'm looking for *new jeans*. / No, thanks. I'm just looking.
I'm *a size 10* / *a small* / *a medium* / *a large*.
Do you have *this/these* in *grey*?
Do you have *this/these* in *a size 10* / *a small*?
Can I try *it/them* on?

3 Complete the dialogues.

1 A: Excuse me, do you have this skirt [1] *in* black?
B: Sorry, we don't.

2 A: Good afternoon. [2] ______ I help you?
B: Yes, please. I'm looking [3] ______ a new winter coat.

3 A: Can I try these trousers [4] ______ ?
B: Of course. The [5] ______ rooms are over there.

4 1.47 **Put the sentences in the dialogue in the correct order. Then listen and check.**

- [ ] Medium.
- [1] This is really cool! Excuse me, do you have this jumper in black?
- [ ] I'm afraid we only have dark blue in medium.
- [ ] The changing rooms are over there.
- [ ] That's a nice colour too.
- [ ] Here you are. Dark blue, medium.
- [ ] Where can I try it on?
- [ ] Yes, we do. What size are you?

5 You are in a clothes shop. Act out the dialogues in pairs. Use the ideas below and add your own.

1 shoes – they're too big
A: *I like these shoes, but they're too big. Do you have them in size 35?*
B: *Sorry, we don't. / Yes, we do. Here you are.*

2 a hoodie – you don't like the colour
A: *This hoodie is OK, but I don't like the colour. Do you have it in blue?*
B: *Sorry, we don't. / Yes, we do. Here you are.*

3 jeans – they're too big
4 a shirt – you don't like the colour
5 trainers – they're too small
6 bag – you don't like the colour

Welcome to Paws Cat Café!

Do you know what a cat café is?
No, it isn't a café for cats. It's a café with cats, where you can have a drink and a snack while you watch them play. You can play with them too!

Here, you can enjoy a cup of *cat-puccino*, tea or a glass of juice while you hang out with our friendly cats. We also serve delicious *cat-cakes*!

Our opening hours are 2 p.m. to 8 p.m. from Tuesday to Friday and 10 a.m. to 8 p.m. on Saturday and Sunday.

Because we don't have many seats, please book before you visit. Saturdays and Sundays are our busiest days, so make sure you book early. Tickets cost £6 per person and you get a free drink with them.

What you need to know before you visit:

- Our visitors must be twelve years old or older.
- You can touch and hold the cats, but please do not carry them around – cats aren't toys.
- When the cats are sleeping, please be patient. Cats are happier and more playful after their sleep.
- Take as many photos as you like, but no flash photos, please.
- Our staff are happy to help you. Just ask!

1 **Have you got a cat? Do you like playing with cats?**

2 1.48 **Listen and read. Choose the best description of the Paws Cat Café.**

a People can take their cats to this café.
b People can play with cats at this café.
c People can buy food for their cats at this café.

3 **Read the text again. Circle T (true) or F (false).**

1 You can drink tea at Paws Cat Café. (T) / F
2 You can have something to eat at the café. T / F
3 The café is open every day. T / F
4 The tickets cost £6. T / F
5 Very young children can come to the café. T / F
6 You can't take photos at the café. T / F

4 **Find the highlighted words in the text. Explain their meaning.**

LOOK! The staff **are** friendly.

5 1.49 **Exam Spot** **Complete the text with the correct form of the words from Exercise 4. Then listen and check.**

The Rose Bush – the coolest new café in town!

The café's [1] *opening hours* are 10 a.m. to 8 p.m., Tuesday to Sunday. A cup of delicious coffee [2] ________ £3 and the second cup is [3] ________ ! The café [4] ________ brilliant meals too. It's busy at lunchtime, but you can [5] ________ a table. The atmosphere is great and the [6] ________ are very helpful.

Fun Spot

6 **Work in pairs. Think of a good idea for a café. Use the questions below to help you. Then present your idea to the class. Have a class vote for the best café.**

1 What's the name of your café?
2 What's special about your café?
3 What are the opening hours?
4 What food and drinks does your café serve?
5 Can you book a table?

Listening and Writing

I can understand opinions and write about my opinions.

1 **Work in pairs. Look at the photos below and guess the answers to the questions.**

Portable speakers

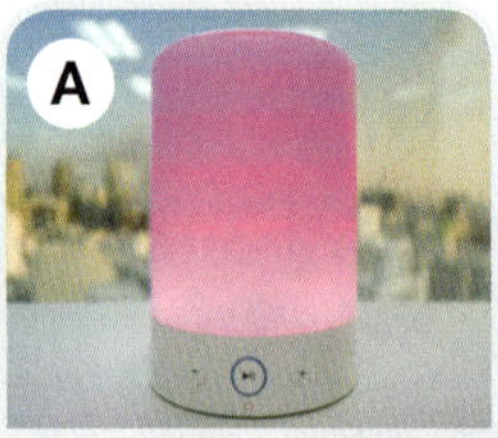

On-the-Glo'

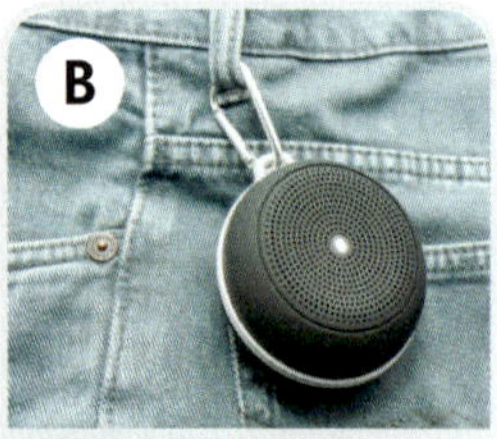

Mini

Sun and Sea

Which portable speaker:

1 is the biggest? ☐
2 is the smallest? ☐
3 is the loudest? ☐
4 is the most expensive? ☐
5 is the cheapest? ☐

2 **1.50 Listen to three people talking about the speakers in Exercise 1. Were your guesses correct?**

3 **1.50 Listen again and circle the correct answer.**

1 Gabby
   a I think the pink one looks really *cool / boring*.
   b Sun and Sea speaker is *better / worse*, because you can take it to the beach.

2 Mark
   a I *think / don't think* the On-the-Glo' speaker has a good design.
   b In my opinion, the Mini speaker is better. You can carry it in your *pocket / bag*.

3 Tim
   a I like the Mini speaker, but it *isn't loud enough / is too loud*.
   b I think the Sun and Sea speaker is *big enough / too big* to carry around.
   c The On-the-Glo' speaker *is / isn't* as small as the Mini, but I don't mind.

4 **Which portable speaker is the best for you? Why?**

5 **Read the email. Which portable charger is better for Mac: the Max Power or the Power Booster? Why?**

	Max Power	Power Booster	Safe Charge
Price	£29.99	£20.99	£15.99
Weight	76 grams	402 grams	140 grams
Size	12x3x2 cm	14x6x3 cm	10x3x2 cm
Ports	2	1	3

Hi Ray,

You want to know about a good portable charger. The Power Booster isn't too bad, but I don't think it's the best choice. It's only got one port and it's too big and heavy. You can't carry it in your pocket. In my opinion, the Max Power is better. First of all, it's got two ports. What's more, it's smaller than the Power Booster. Finally, it's lighter. It's more expensive than the Power Booster, but I don't mind.

Cheers, Mac

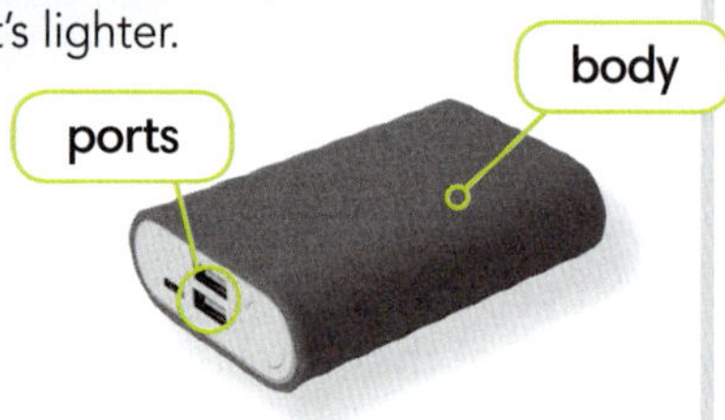

6 **Read the Writing box. Find the words *First of all*, *What's more* and *Finally* in the email in Exercise 5.**

Writing Ordering arguments

You can use *First of all*, *What's more* and *Finally* when you want to give a number of reasons for your opinion.

7 **Writing Time Look at Exercise 5. Write an email to Ray about the Max Power and the Safe Charge.**

Find ideas

What is good/bad about each portable charger?

Draft

Write the email. Give your opinion of the portable chargers and say which one is better. Give three arguments.

Hi Ray,
You want to know …
I think … / I don't think … *In my opinion, …*
First of all, … *What's more, …* *Finally, …*

Check and write

Remember to use *First of all*, *What's more* and *Finally* to give reasons for your opinion. Write the final version of your email.

Vocabulary

1 Complete the text with the words in the box.

carry cash cashier change ~~list~~
queue receipt trolley

We go to the supermarket every week. Mum has a shopping [1] *list* with the things she wants to buy. We put our shopping in the [2] ________ and then we go and stand in a [3] ________ . Mum pays for the shopping in [4] ________ and the [5] ________ gives her the [6] ________ . Mum takes the [7] ________ and puts it in her bag with the change. Then, we [8] ________ the shopping to the car and go home.

2 Look at the pictures and write the words.

1 s*ports* s*hop*

2 b________

3 b________

4 n________

5 g________

6 c________

Pronunciation

3 1.51 Listen and repeat: /ɒ/ or /ɔː/?

There are friendly shop assistants.
There are baskets on the floor.
And a lot of special offers,
in the new department store.

Grammar

4 Complete the sentences with the comparative form and *than* or the superlative form of the adjectives.

1 The blue skirt is *longer than* (long) this black one.
2 Today is ________ (hot) day of the year. It's 38°C!
3 I'm a bad cook, but my brother is ________ (bad) me.
4 The first and second exercises were ________ (easy) the third and fourth ones.
5 I think Science is ________ (interesting) subject.
6 Their house is ________ (modern) our house.
7 Who is ________ (good) singer in the world?

5 Complete the sentences with one word in each gap.

1 Simon is 1.65 metres tall and Luke is 1.63 metres. Luke isn't as tall *as* Simon.
2 I can't buy these jeans. They're ________ expensive.
3 Is the water warm ________ ? I want to go swimming.
4 Jim is talented and Lee is talented too, but is Lee ________ talented as Jim?
5 I don't like this painting. The colours are ________ dark.
6 The apples are cheap, but they aren't ________ cheap as the oranges.
7 I can't play basketball. I'm not tall ________ .
8 I don't like my town. It's ________ quiet for me.

Communication

6 1.52 Complete the dialogue with sentences a–f. Then listen and check.

a Can I help you?
b Can I try it on?
c Do you have it in blue?
d I'm looking for a new jacket.
e The changing rooms are over there.
f What size are you? Medium or large?

Assistant: Good morning. [1] *a*
Stuart: Yes, please. [2] ___ I like this one, but I'm not sure about the colour. [3] ___
Assistant: Yes, we do. [4] ___
Stuart: Large.
Assistant: Here you are.
Stuart: [5] ___
Assistant: Yes, of course. [6] ___
Stuart: Thank you.

Check yourself!

- I can talk about shopping. ☐
- I can use comparative and superlative adjectives. ☐
- I can use *too*, *not … enough* and *(not) as … as*. ☐
- I can buy clothes. ☐

Reading and Writing

1 Is shopping one of your chores? What other chores do you do at home? Tell a partner.

2 **Exam Spot** Read the text. Circle the correct answer a, b or c.

TEEN SHOPPING

Here are the results of our class survey about shopping. Find out what the girls and boys said!

First of all, we discovered that most girls love shopping [1] ___ clothes. A lot of boys enjoy shopping for clothes too, [2] ___ they say they are too busy to stand in queues. So, what [3] ___ boys like buying? A lot of boys say that sports shops are the [4] ___ interesting. They agree small sports shops are sometimes [5] ___ expensive, but some of them say that the shop assistants are usually friendlier [6] ___ they are in big shops. Both girls and boys love [7] ___ the latest technology. They think big shops are [8] ___ than smaller shops because they are often cheaper.

Finally, all students from our class love helping their parents buy things online. They agree it isn't [9] ___ expensive as shopping in a traditional shop and it's more fun!

	a	b	c
1	a the	b to	(c) for
2	a so	b as	c but
3	a do	b does	c are
4	a very	b worse	c most
5	a much	b enough	c too
6	a that	b than	c and
7	a buying	b buys	c buy
8	a best	b better	c good
9	a as	b enough	c very

3 **Exam Spot** Write 60–80 words about your shopping habits. Use these questions to help you.

1 How often to do go shopping?
2 Where do you go?
3 Who do you go with?
4 What do you like buying?
5 What's your favourite shop? Why?

I often go shopping (at the weekend …)
I usually go to (town / the shopping centre …)
I go with … / I love buying …
My favourite shop is … because …

4 **Exam Spot** Complete Mark's blog post with one word in each gap.

Mark's blog

Mum [1] *is* visiting an old school friend in France this week, so my sister, Dad [2] ______ I have more chores. I always [3] ______ the table before dinner, but this week I also need to clear it after the meals and [4] ______ the dishwasher when the dishes are clean. What's more, I have to iron my clothes. I'm really busy, but my chores are better [5] ______ my sister's. Right now, she is hanging [6] ______ the washing. I hate that chore!

Listening

5 **Exam Spot** 1.53 Listen and complete the sentences.

1 The new café is *modern* .
2 The Sandwich Café doesn't have a ________ .
3 Right now, students from Class ________ are making sandwiches.
4 The chefs from the school ________ do t
shopping.
5 Laura thinks making sandwiches is the most ________ job.
6 The opening hours are from ________ p.m. to 5.30 p.m.

Communication

6 **Exam Spot** **Look at the pictures. Match a–h to 1–6. There are two extra sentences.**

a Can you feed Bobby? He's hungry.
b Do you need any help with lunch, Mum?
c Here you are, size 8.
d Yes, of course. The changing rooms are over there.
e No, thanks. I'm just looking.
f Can I try these clothes on?
g Can you help me clear the table?
h Anna says there's a special offer in the clothes shop!

7 **Exam Spot** **Ask and answer the questions in pairs.**

1 Do you like going to the supermarket?
2 Are you messy or organised?
3 What do you like doing with your family?
4 What types of shops do you usually visit?
5 Are you sometimes too busy to do things you like?

Exam Language Bank

Household chores

clear the table	make your bed
empty the dishwasher	put away your clothes
feed the dog	set the table
hang out the washing	take out the rubbish
iron your T-shirt	vacuum your room
load the dishwasher / washing machine	water the plants

Personality adjectives

bossy	loud	organised	quiet
easy-going	messy	patient	tidy

Shopping

cashier	check the price
shopping bag	get a receipt
shopping basket	get your change
shopping list	pay by card
shopping trolley	pay for the shopping
special offer	pay in cash
carry the shopping	stand in a queue

Shops

baker's	clothes shop	newsagent's
bookshop	department store	shoe shop
chemist's	greengrocer's	sports shop

Asking for and offering help

Asking for help
Can you help me *with the sofa*, please?
Can you *move the coffee table*, please?
Reacting
No problem. / Yes, of course.
I'm sorry, I can't. I'm *busy right now*.
Offering help
Can I help you *with the lamp*?
Do you need any help *with the lamp*?
Reacting
Yes, please. / No, that's fine, thank you.

Shopping for clothes

Shop assistant
Can I help you?
What size are you?
Yes, we do. Here you are. / Sorry, we don't.
The changing rooms are over there.
Customer
I'm looking for *new jeans*. / No thanks. I'm just looking.
I'm *a size 10 / a small / a medium / a large*.
Do you have *this/these* in *grey / a size 10 / a small*?
Can I try *it/them* on?

3 Going on holiday

Vocabulary I can talk about holiday activities.

In this unit

Vocabulary
- Going on holiday
- Phrases with *get*

Grammar
- Past Simple affirmative and negative
- Past Simple questions and short answers

13–14

3.2 Grammar video

15

3.2 Grammar animation

16

3.3 Grammar animation

17

3.4 Communication video

18

BBC Culture video

I know that!

1 **What do people usually do on holiday? Match the words to make expressions.**

~~buy~~ do go read stay visit

a guidebook a museum ~~a souvenir~~ in a hotel sightseeing water sports

buy a souvenir

Julie Reed and her parents are planning their next holiday. This summer they would like to go to Crete, an island in Greece.

2 2.1 **Listen and repeat. Look at page 34. What would the Reed family like to do on holiday?**

Vocabulary Going on holiday

explore an area / a city / a town go camping go cycling go hiking go on a boat trip go on a day trip go on a guided tour go snorkelling go to the beach try the local food

Julie would like to …

3 2.2 **Listen to the Reed family and check your answers to Exercise 2.**

4 Match 1–5 to a–e.

1 [c] When you explore an area,
2 [ ] When you go snorkelling,
3 [ ] When you go camping,
4 [ ] When you go on a day trip,
5 [ ] When you go to the beach,

a you can see what's under the water.
b you sleep in a tent.
c you walk around and learn about it.
d you often have sand in your shoes.
e you leave in the morning and return in the evening.

5 Exam Spot **Complete the text. Use the Vocabulary box to help you.**

Crete – the perfect place for a holiday!

- You can [1] *go* to the beach every day, swim and go [2]_______ in the clean blue water.
- You can also go on a boat [3]_______ to some small islands near Crete.
- Do you enjoy walking? You can go [4]_______ in the mountains.
- Are you interested in history? You can go on a guided [5]_______ and see famous places like Knossos or you can [6]_______ old towns, like Rethymnon and Chania.
- And of course, you can try the local [7]_______. It's delicious.

Knossos

6 2.3 **What are the Reed family doing today? Listen and match the days to the activities.**

~~Monday~~ Tuesday Wednesday Thursday Friday

a They're at the beach. _______
b They're trying the local food. _______
c They're going on a day trip. _______
d They're going camping. _______
e They're exploring an old town. *Monday*

7 Read the comments and write suggestions using the activities in the Vocabulary box.

1 I love swimming and looking at the animals in the sea.
Why don't you go snorkelling?
2 I don't want to stay in a hotel.
3 I love walking in the mountains.
4 I want someone to tell me about the famous places.
5 I like sitting in the sand and looking at the sea.

8 Act out the dialogues from Exercise 7 in pairs.

9 In pairs, finish the sentences.

1 You need special clothes or equipment to …
go snorkelling, …
2 In the city you can …
3 When you go to the seaside you can …

I remember that!

10 Make a list of five activities you would like to do on holiday. Start with the one you would like to do most. Then compare your lists in small groups.

1 go on a boat trip
2 try the local food
3 go hiking
4 go to the beach
5 go camping

I can use the Past Simple in affirmative and negative sentences.

I didn't know that

The Nicholses are going away on holiday today.

Dad: Come on, everyone! We have a plane to catch! … Angela, where are the passports?
Mum: Well, they were on the stairs a few minutes ago.
Dad: Here they are! Sorry, I didn't see them. I'm putting them in the … Why's the rubbish still here? George? I asked you to take out the rubbish an hour ago!

Dad: The rubbish was your job, young man! It wasn't mine!
George: Sorry, Dad, I didn't hear that.
Dad: Oh, forget it!

Dad: That's weird! I'm sure I closed that suitcase last night.
Harry: My backpack was full, so I took out some of my stuff and put it in that suitcase.
Dad: What on earth is this?
Harry: It's my pillow. You know I can't sleep without it.
Dad: No, I didn't know that. Take it with you on the plane … Angela, don't forget to lock the back door, OK? Give me a hand, boys!

Finally, they got into the taxi and left for the airport.

Dad: Oh, no!

1 13 2.4 **Watch or listen and read. How are the Nicholses going to the airport?**

2 Read the story. Circle the correct answer.

1 Dad is looking for the *passports* / *rubbish*.
2 They were *on the stairs* / *in the kitchen*.
3 It was *Harry's* / *George's* job to take out the rubbish.
4 *Harry* / *Dad* put the pillow in the suitcase.
5 Dad asks Harry to take *the suitcase* / *the pillow* with him on the plane.

3 2.5 **Listen and repeat. Find these expressions in the story.**

Say it!

That's weird! What on earth …?

4 **Guess!** **What's wrong? Have a class vote.**

a Mrs Nichols forgot to lock the back door.
b They left their passports at home.

5 14 2.6 **Now watch or listen and check.**

Grammar
Past Simple affirmative and negative

+	–
to be	
I/He/She/It **was** here.	I/He/She/It **wasn't** here.
We/You/They **were** here.	We/You/They **weren't** here.
Regular verbs	
I/You/He/She/It **closed** it.	I/You/He/She/It **didn't close** it.
We/You/They **closed** it.	We/You/They **didn't close** it.
Irregular verbs	
I/You/He/She/It **heard** that.	I/You/He/She/It **didn't hear** that.
We/You/They **heard** that.	We/You/They **didn't hear** that.
Time expressions	
yesterday, last night, last Tuesday, last month, last year	
a few minutes ago, an hour ago, a week ago, a year ago	

15 Get Grammar!

6 Look at the story on page 36. Complete the text with *was*, *wasn't*, *were* or *weren't*.

At the beginning, Mum and the boys [1]*were* in the house, but they [2]_______ in the hall. The passports [3]_______ on the stairs. The rubbish bag [4]_______ in the hall too and Dad [5]_______ happy. He [6]_______ surprised because Harry's pillow [7]_______ in the grey suitcase.

7 2.7 Write the infinitives of these irregular verbs. Then listen and check.

drank gave got had left met put
read spent swam took went

drink – drank

8 Complete Harry's blog post with the Past Simple form of the verbs.

Yesterday, I [1]*didn't get up* (not get up) early so I [2]_________ (not have) breakfast at the hotel. But later in the day, Dad and I [3]_________ (explore) the area and we [4]_________ (try) the local cheese pie. We [5]_________ (love) it! George and Mum [6]_________ (go) to the beach. They [7]_________ (not swim) because they [8]_________ (not have) their towels with them.

9 2.8 Complete the sentences with the Past Simple form of the verbs. Then number the sentences. Listen and check.

a ☐ The weather [1]*wasn't* (not be) good. We [2]_________ (spend) all the time inside our tents and [3]_________ (drink) tea to keep warm.

b ☐ I [4]_________ (not have) much fun, but I [5]_________ (read) three interesting books!

c [*1*] Last summer, my parents [6]_________ (want) to go camping, so we [7]_________ (go) to the Lake District.

d ☐ On the last day, it finally [8]_________ (stop) raining. But I [9]_________ (be) happy to go home!

Fun Spot

10 Game! Play as a class. Take turns to make sentences.

A: *When I was on holiday last year, I went cycling.*

B: *I didn't go cycling, but I tried the local food.*

C: *I didn't try the local food, but I …*

Doctor Q The film premiere

Doctor Q and Rob are back from a trip. They went to a big film premiere.

Millie: How was your trip?
Rob: It was great!
Millie: Was the weather good?
Rob: No, it wasn't. On Friday, it rained all day. On Saturday, it was very windy and on Sunday …
Pi: And the film? Was it good? Did people like it?
Dr Q: Yes, it was and yes, they did.
Pi: Did you go to the party after the film?
Rob: Yes, we did!

Pi: Wow! Did you meet any film stars?
Rob: Yes, we did. We met Brian Gosley.
Pi: Really? Did you talk to him?
Dr Q: Yes, Pi, we did!
Pi: What did he say?
Dr Q: 'Hello, pleased to meet you.'
Pi: Oh, just that? Did you take any photos?
Rob: I didn't.
Dr Q: But I did. Look!

Pi: That's not Brian Gosley! That's food! Why did you take a photo of food?!
Dr Q: Because it was fantastic!
Pi: Oh …

1 Look at picture 1. Where was the film premiere?

2 2.9 Listen and read. Who is Brian Gosley?

3 Read the sentences. Circle T (true) or F (false).

1 Rob didn't like the weather. (T) / F
2 The film premiere was a success. T / F
3 Doctor Q didn't go to the party. T / F
4 Doctor Q had a long chat with Brian Gosley. T / F
5 Doctor Q didn't take any photos at the party. T / F

Grammar
Past Simple questions and short answers

▶ 16 Get Grammar!

?	Short answers
to be	
Was I/he/she/it good?	Yes, I/he/she/it **was**. No, I/he/she/it **wasn't**.
Were we/you/they good?	Yes, we/you/they **were**. No, we/you/they **weren't**.
Regular and irregular verbs	
Did I/you/he/she/it **like** it? **Did** I/you/he/she/it **meet** Brian?	Yes, I/you/he/she/it/ **did**. No, I/you/he/she/it **didn't**.
Did we/you/they **like** it? **Did** we/you/they **meet** Brian?	Yes, we/you/they **did**. No, we/you/they **didn't**.

Where **was** the film premiere? What **did** he **say**?

4 🔊 **2.10 Pi asked a lot more questions. Write Doctor Q's short answers. Then listen and check. Complete the last sentence.**

1 **Pi:** Were you and Rob on time for the film?
Dr Q: ✔ *Yes, we were.*

2 **Pi:** Did you go by taxi?
Dr Q: ✔ ________

3 **Pi:** Was the film very long?
Dr Q: ✘ ________

4 **Pi:** Did Brian Gosley give you his autograph?
Dr Q: ✘ ________

5 **Pi:** Were you and Rob tired after the party?
Dr Q: ✘ ________

6 **Pi:** Did you bring me a present from London?
Dr Q: ✔ ________ . It's a ________ .

5 The robots are talking about Millie and Pi's weekend. Write Rob's questions.

1 what / you and Pi / do / on Saturday?
What did you and Pi do on Saturday?
2 what film / you / see?
3 it / be / good?
4 Pi / eat / popcorn?
5 what / you / do / after the cinema?
6 Pi's friends / be / at the cinema too?

6 **Exam Spot** 🔊 **2.11 Match the questions in Exercise 5 to answers a–g. There is one extra answer. Then listen and check.**

a ☐ No, it wasn't. It was silly.
b ☐ *Crazy Animals 3*.
c ☐ Yes, he did. He loves it!
d [*1*] We went to the cinema too.
e ☐ Yes, we did.
f ☐ No, they weren't. We had a picnic in the park.
g ☐ We met Pi's friends.

7 Imagine you want to ask your friend about a film premiere he/she went to. Complete the questions.

Did you like ~~Were~~ Was What

1 *Were* you excited?
2 ________ film did you see?
3 Did you ________ the film?
4 ________ the cinema big?
5 ________ you see any film stars?
6 Did ________ take any photos?

Fun Spot

8 Work in pairs. Ask and answer the questions in Exercise 7.

Can you bring me my phone?

George and Harry are waiting for Mum at the hotel lobby.

Harry: Can I have the tablet now?
George: Sorry, you can't. I'm using it at the moment.
Mum: Boys, can one of you bring me my phone, please? It's upstairs. Oh, and the guidebook.
George: Sorry, Mum. I can't quit the game now.
Harry: Yes, Mum, no problem.
Mum: Thank you, darling. I'm going to be outside with Dad.
Harry: Mum, the room key! … Oh, never mind.
Receptionist: Can I help you?
Harry: Yes, please. Could you give me the key to Room 217?
Receptionist: Yes, of course. Here you are.
Harry: Thank you.
George: Harry, can you get my sunglasses too?
Harry: Sorry, I can't hear you!

1 17 2.12 **Watch or listen and read. What does George want from the room?**

2 2.13 **Listen and repeat.**

Communication Requests

Making requests

Can you *bring me my phone*, please?
Could you *give me the key to my room*?
Can I *have the tablet*?

Responding to requests

Yes, no problem. / Yes, of course.
Sorry, I/you can't. *I'm using it right now.*
Not now, sorry. *I'm busy.*

3 2.14 **Complete the dialogues with one word in each gap. Then listen and check.**

1 A: [1] *Could* you bring me my bag, [2] ________ ?
B: Yes, of [3] ________ . Where is it?
2 A: Can [4] ________ borrow some money from you?
B: Yes, no [5] ________ .
3 A: Can you give me the train timetable, please?
B: [6] ________ , I can't. I can't find it.
4 A: Can you help me with my homework?
B: [7] ________ now, sorry. I'm busy.

4 In pairs, make and respond to requests. Use the ideas below and add your own.

1 you / give / your smartphone / check the train times ✔
A: *Could you give me your smartphone, please? I need to check the train times.*
B: *Yes, of course.*
2 I / borrow / some money from you / buy some souvenirs ✘
3 you / take / photo of us ✘
4 I / close / the window / it's cold ✔

5 Exam Spot 2.15 **The Brett family are going home after their holiday. What are they looking/asking for? Listen and match people 1–4 to objects A–F. There are two extra objects.**

1 *B* Laura
2 ☐ Sam
3 ☐ Dad
4 ☐ Mum

A

B

C

D

E

F

My Alaskan holiday

by Shirley Burns

A

My family and I don't like going to the beach. We get bored there, so last summer we went to Alaska for our holidays. Alaska is the biggest state of the USA and one of the last wild places on Earth. It has volcanoes and mountains, rivers, thousands of islands and more than three million lakes! It's never very hot there, but the days are long in July and it gets dark late.

B

We went to Juneau, the capital of Alaska, by plane. There, we joined a group of three other families and two guides. We travelled around the country in caravans, and we camped in a different place every night. The caravans had beds and bathrooms and were very comfortable! At night it got cold, so we sat around the camp fire and ate our food.

C

We had a fantastic time. We went kayaking, fishing and hiking in the mountains. We always had a guide with us, so we didn't get lost. The forests were full of wild animals and we saw a wolf and grizzly bears. We got tired because there were so many activities, but we loved it. The last day of our holiday was the best! We went on a boat trip and saw humpback whales!

1 2.16 **Read and listen to the text. Match paragraphs A–C to headings 1–4. There is one extra heading.**

1 ☐ A dangerous place
2 ☐ Life on the road
3 ☐ An unusual place for a holiday
4 ☐ Not a holiday for lazy people!

2 **I know that!** **Which geographical features does Alaska have? Which of them can you see in the photo?**

forest island lake mountain river sea volcano

3 **Read the text again. Which paragraph:**

1 *B* mentions the name of a city?
2 ☐ mentions very big numbers?
3 ☐ describes Shirley's favourite part of the holiday?
4 ☐ says how Shirley travelled around Alaska?
5 ☐ says why Shirley and her family went to Alaska?
6 ☐ names the animals Shirley saw?

4 **Would you like to go on a holiday to Alaska? Why? / Why not?**

5 2.17 **Listen and repeat. Find these phrases in the text.**

Vocabulary Phrases with *get*

get bored get cold get dark get lost get tired

6 **Complete the sentences with a word from the Vocabulary box.**

1 I didn't take a map with me and I got *lost* in the city.
2 I need a jumper. It's getting ________ !
3 This film isn't interesting and I'm getting ________ .
4 In the winter in the UK it gets ________ at four o'clock.
5 After a long walk, we got ________ and decided to have a rest.

3.6 Listening and Writing

I can understand and write texts describing holidays.

1 Look at the photos. Which place would you like to visit on holiday? Compare with a friend.

2 2.18 Listen and match speakers 1–4 to the places in Exercise 1.

1 [*B*] Sandra
2 [ ] Derek
3 [ ] Alicia
4 [ ] Ian

3 2.18 Listen again. Complete the blog post with one word in each gap.

Our Class Blog

Sandra
My family and I went to Rome in August. I made a lot of [1] *friends* and I loved the food! I didn't like sightseeing very much because I got [2] ________ .

Derek
Last summer we went to my grandparents' [3] ________ . It was a great holiday and we loved looking after the [4] ________ .

Alice
Our holiday in Jamaica was the best holiday of my life! Jamaica is a beautiful [5] ________ and we did a lot of water [6] ________ there.

Ian
We go to our Dad's village in [7] ________ every year. I wanted to go swimming, but the water in the [8] ________ was very cold!

4 Read Derek's email. Who is he writing to?

(1) Dear Aunt Carol,
I hope you're well. Lilian and I are having a lovely time in the village!
I wish you were here!

(2) There are lots of things to do here. Last Friday we went fishing with Grandad. We sat next to the river for hours. I caught one fish, Lilian caught two and Grandad caught three!
Yesterday we went hiking in the mountains. Lilian and I got tired, but Grandad didn't get tired at all. He's fit!

(3) I need to help Granny with the animals now, so I can't write any more.
Lots of love,
Derek

5 Read the Writing box. Which of the expressions can you find in Derek's email?

Writing A holiday email

1. **At the beginning** write: *Hi/Hello …* (to a friend) or *Dear …* (to an older person you know).
   You can also write: *How are you? I hope you're well. We're having a lovely time … I wish you were here.*
2. **In the middle**, describe your holiday.
3. **At the end**, you can write: *I need to …, so I can't write any more.*
   You can add: *See you soon* or *Love / Lots of love.*
   Remember to write your name.

6 Writing Time Imagine you are on holiday. Write an email to a friend or someone from your family and tell him/her about it.

Find ideas
Make notes about your holiday. Use these questions to help you.
Where are you and who is with you?
What did you do last week / yesterday?
Why do you need to stop writing? (optional)

Draft
Write your email. Use the Writing box to help you.

Check and write
Make sure you begin and end your email correctly. Write the final version of your email.

Vocabulary

1 Complete the texts with the words in the box.

beach boat camping ~~explore~~
guided hiking snorkelling trip try

We're in Vienna and we want to see the city. We can [1] *explore* it on our own or we can go on a [2] ________ tour. I also want to [3] ________ the local food.

I want to go [4] ________ . We can sleep under the stars and go [5] ________ in the mountains.

Let's go on a day [6] ________ to the country and tomorrow we can go on a [7] ________ trip to an island.

It's hot today. Let's go to the [8] ________ . We can sit in the sun or go swimming and [9] ________ in the sea.

2 Complete the sentences with one word in each gap.

1 Winter is coming and it's getting *cold* .
2 I don't like playing computer games. I get ________ .
3 Can we stop and have a rest? I'm getting ________ .
4 Where's the map? I don't want to get ________ .
5 I turned on the lights when it got ________ .

Grammar

3 Complete the page of Sue's diary with the correct Past Simple form of the verbs in brackets.

10th August

I [1] *arrived* (arrive) here five days ago. It [2] ________ (be) fantastic to see Aunt Kate, Uncle Joe, Alfie and Lulu. We [3] ________ (not sleep) a lot. We [4] ________ (talk) all night, but we [5] ________ (not be) tired in the morning!

Yesterday we [6] ________ (go) cycling near the lake. We [7] ________ (have) a picnic, but we [8] ________ (not go) swimming. In the evening, Alfie and I [9] ________ (play) a computer game and Lulu [10] ________ (read) a comic book. I love it here!

4 In your notebook, write questions and answers.

1 Dad / cook / spaghetti / last night? ✔
Did Dad cook spaghetti last night?
Yes, he did.
2 the weather / be / warm and sunny? ✘
3 the students / like / their new teacher? ✔
4 you / know / everyone at the party? ✘
5 they / be / at school / two days ago? ✘
6 you and Sam / buy / these souvenirs / yesterday? ✔

Pronunciation

5 2.19 Listen and repeat: /ð/ or /d/.

My father was there, my mother and Jade.
It rained, so we stayed at home and we played.

Communication

6 2.20 Complete the dialogues. Then listen and check.

1 A: [1]C*a n* you drive me to the town centre?
B: Not now, [2]s_ _ _ _ . I'm very busy.
2 A: [3]C_ _ _ _ you [4]b_ _ _ _ me my laptop, please? It's in my room.
B: Yes, of [5]c_ _ _ _ _ .
3 A: Can you [6]g_ _ _ me the map, [7]p_ _ _ _ _ ?
B: Yes, no [8]p_ _ _ _ _ _ . Here it is.

Check yourself! ✔

- I can talk about holiday activities. ☐
- I can use the Past Simple. ☐
- I can make and respond to requests. ☐

Get Culture! A journey around the USA

Choose a continent: North America Choose a country: United States

The United States of America is the third largest country in the world. Its neighbours are Canada in the north and Mexico in the south. It has the Atlantic Ocean in the east and the Pacific Ocean in the west.

Fifty states make up the United States. Two of them, Alaska and Hawaii, are outside the main territory. The capital city of the USA is Washington DC, and the top three largest cities are New York, Los Angeles and Chicago.

The landscape of the USA is beautiful and varied. In the southwest, we find the Rocky Mountains and the Colorado River 1. The mountains continue into the west, where you can also find the Mojave Desert 2 (the hottest desert in North America) and three world famous national parks: Yosemite 3, Yellowstone and Redwood 4. In Redwood, you can see some of the world's tallest trees!

The northeast has the Great Lakes 5. The southeast has the Mississippi River (the fourth longest river in the world) and the Everglades wetlands 6, where you can find hundreds of different types of animals and plants.

1 **What do you know about the USA? In small groups, think of three facts. Compare your ideas as a class.**

2 **2.21 Read and listen to the text about the USA. Answer the questions.**

1 Which countries are USA's neighbours?
2 Which ocean is west of the USA?
3 How many states are there in the USA?
4 Which city is larger – Washington or Chicago?
5 How many rivers are mentioned in the text?
6 Which is the hottest desert in North America?

3 **2.22 Listen to three young Americans talking about their holidays. Complete the table.**

Person/ holiday	1 Kelly Hawaii Island	2 Adam Everglades, Florida	3 Isabella Rocky Mountains
Geography	rain forests, [1] *beaches*, volcanoes	wetlands with grass, [3] ________	mountains, [5] ________, [6] ________
Activities	[2] ________, golf	taking photos, [4] ______ rides	hiking, [7] ________

4 **Where do you go on holiday and what do you do? What activities do you like doing? What don't you like doing?**

Yellowstone and the Grand Canyon

BBC

A 18 **Watch the video and answer the presenter's questions. Which places does the video talk about?**

Redwood	Arizona	the Mississipi River	the Colorado River
the Rocky Mountains	the Mojave Desert		

B 18 **Watch the video again. Answer the questions.**

Yellowstone National Park

1. Which part of the USA is it in?
2. What is the name of the river that runs through it?
3. How many geysers are there in it?

The Grand Canyon National Park

4. Which state is it in?
5. How long is the Grand Canyon?
6. What is the hottest temperature in the summer?

C **Which of the two national parks would you like to visit? Why? What would you like to do there?**

PROJECT

- **Work in groups. Make a digital presentation of a famous national park in your country.**
- **Plan your presentation. Decide who searches the Internet for interesting information, who looks for the photos and pictures, etc.**
- **Write about the national park. Use these questions to help you.**

  Where is it?
  What geographical features does it have?
  What plants and animals live there?
  What can visitors do there?

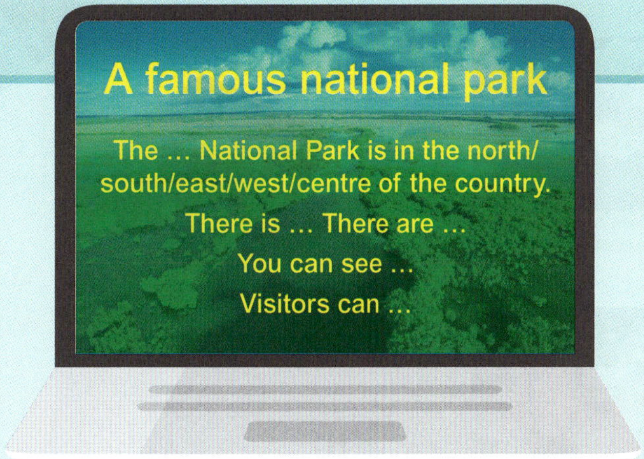

- **Put your texts and photos together.**
- **Show your presentation to the class. Which is your favourite presentation? Why?**

4 Useful things

Vocabulary

I can talk about useful objects powered by electricity.

In this unit

Vocabulary
- Useful things
- Using technology
- Smartphones

Grammar
- Past Continuous
- Past Continuous and Past Simple with *when*
- Adverbs of manner

19–20 4.2 Grammar video

21 4.2 Grammar animation

22 4.3 Grammar animation

23 4.4 Communication video

I know that!

1 Complete the technology words and add your own. Do you use these items every day?

1 fr_dg_	**3** pr_nt_r	**5** t_bl_t
2 c_m_r_	**4** scr_ _n	**6** m_b_l_ ph_n_

A

B

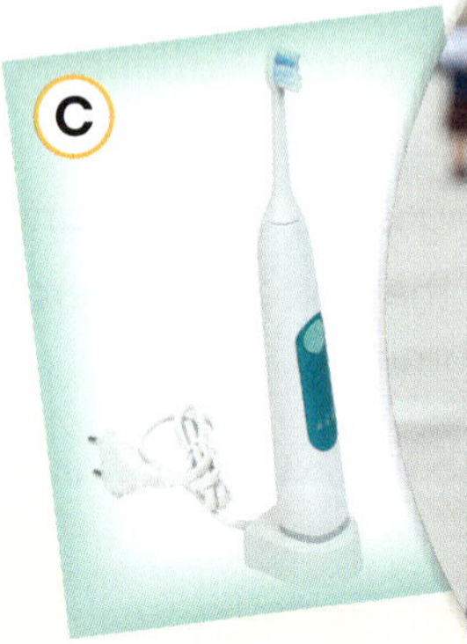

C

D

E

F

G

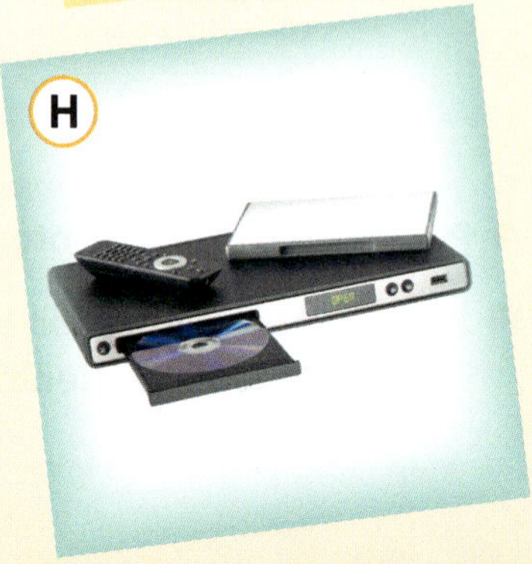

H

I

J

2 2.23 **Listen and repeat. Look at the photos on page 46 and match the objects to the words in the Vocabulary box.**

Vocabulary Useful things

blender DVD player electric toothbrush games console hairdryer microwave oven remote control smart TV toaster USB stick

3 Exam Spot **Read the definitions. Write the words.**

You use it to …

1 dry your hair after you wash it. *hairdryer*
2 make a drink with fruit and vegetables. __________
3 keep your documents and photos. __________
4 change the channels without touching your TV set. __________
5 play games. __________
6 warm up or cook food. __________

4 Game! Play *Three Questions*.

A: *Is it in the kitchen?*
B: *No, it isn't.*
A: *Is it in the bathroom?*
B: *Sometimes.*
A: *Do you use it on your hair?*
B: *Yes, you do.*
A: *It's a hairdryer!*
B: *That's right!*

5 2.24 **Listen to four interviews. What is each person talking about? Use words from the Vocabulary box.**

1 *remote control*
2 __________
3 __________
4 __________

6 2.24 **Listen again. Why can't the speakers in Exercise 5 live without these items? Complete the sentences.**

1 Because she doesn't want to get up and *change the channels* .
2 Because he always has __________ .
3 Because she needs to __________ after __________ at work.
4 Because he isn't __________ when he's __________ .

7 2.25 **Listen and repeat. Label the pictures with the verbs in the Vocabulary box.**

Vocabulary Using technology

plug in unplug turn on turn off

1 *turn on*

2 __________

3 __________

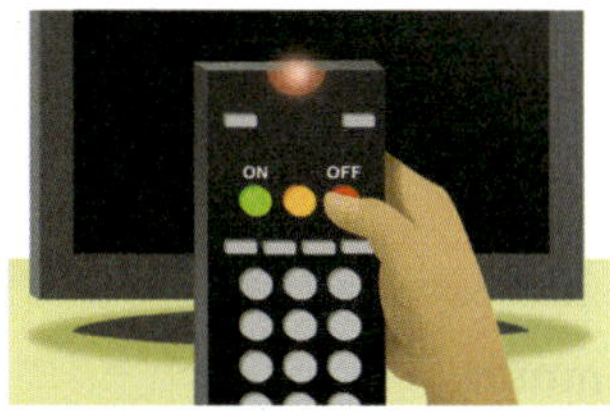

4 __________

8 Complete the sentences with one word in each gap. Use the Vocabulary box in Exercise 7 to help you.

1 Press ⏻ to turn [1] *on* the TV when you are ready to watch. Press it again to [2] __________ off the TV when you want to stop watching.
2 Always be careful when you [3] __________ in the hairdryer. Make sure your hands are not wet. Never [4] __________ the hairdryer while it is in use.
3 First, turn [5] __________ the toaster and then unplug it. Clean it. After that, plug it [6] __________ again to make toast.

I remember that!

9 How often do you use the things in Exercise 2? Complete the table in your notebook.

never	*hairdryer*
2–4 times a week	*toaster*
every day	*remote control*

10 Compare your answers in pairs. Tell the class.

Lisa uses a hairdryer three times a week.
I never use a hairdryer.
Nico uses the TV remote control every day.
I do too.

Harry was playing tennis

1

2

Emma: Hi.
Poppy: Hi.
George: Check this out!
Poppy: Is that a selfie with Adrianna? The pop star? You're kidding!
George: No, I'm not! Honest!
Emma: Yesterday afternoon, about four o'clock, we were hanging out in the park. That's where we saw Adrianna!
George: Harry wasn't with us, because he was playing tennis.
Poppy: What was Adrianna doing in our park? Was she jogging?
Emma: No, she wasn't. She was there with a film crew. They were filming the video for her new song.
George: We talked to her and took some photos.
Poppy: And I wasn't there! That's not fair!

3

Emma: You were at home. You were studying.
Poppy: No, I wasn't studying. I was at the shops with Mum. We were looking for a new hairdryer. Aargh! Stupid hairdryer!
Emma: Harry's also very upset. He's a big fan!
George: You know what? I think I can do something about that … I just need to download an app first …

1 19 2.26 **Watch or listen and read. Who's the woman in the photo with Emma and George?**

2 Read the story. Complete the sentences.

1 George is showing Poppy a *photo* on his phone.
2 Harry __________ with George and Emma when they saw the pop star.
3 The film crew were making a music __________ .
4 George and Emma __________ to Adrianna.
5 Harry is Adrianna's __________ .

3 2.27 **Listen and repeat. Find the expressions in the story.**

Say it!

Check this out! You're kidding! Honest!

4 Guess! **What's George's idea? Work in pairs. Make a guess.**

5 20 2.28 **Now watch or listen and check.**

Grammar Past Continuous

+	−
I/He/She/It **was studying**.	I/He/She/It **wasn't studying**.
You/We/They **were studying**.	You/We/They **weren't studying**.
?	**Short answers**
Was I/he/she/it **studying**?	Yes, I/he/she/it **was**. No, I/he/she/it **wasn't**.
Were you/we/they **studying**?	Yes, you/we/they **were**. No, you/we/they **weren't**.

What **was** Adrianna **doing** at four o'clock?

Where **were** they **filming** the music video?

Time expressions

at eight o'clock, ten minutes ago

21 Get Grammar!

6 Complete Harry's blog post with the Past Continuous form of the verbs.

At four o'clock yesterday, Emma and George [1] *were hanging out* (hang out) in the park. Adrianna was in the park too! She [2] ______ (film) a new video there. At four o'clock the cameramen [3] ______ (eat) sandwiches and Adrianna wasn't busy! I wasn't in the park because I [4] ______ (play) tennis. Poppy wasn't there either. Poppy and her mum [5] ______ (look) for a new hairdryer at the shopping centre!

7 In your notebook, write sentences about what was happening at 7 p.m. yesterday.

1 Poppy / take a photo of Emma ✗ take a selfie ✓
Poppy wasn't taking a photo of Emma.
She was taking a selfie.

2 George and Harry / make sandwiches ✗ make popcorn ✓

3 Emma / use a blender ✗ use a toaster ✓

4 Gran / look for her glasses ✗ look for the remote control ✓

8 2.29 **Exam Spot** What were they doing? Listen to the dialogue and match the names to the people and the dog in the picture. There is one extra name.

Beth | Frank | Bob

Kate | Jane | Chris

9 In your notebook, write questions about the people and the dog in Exercise 8. Ask and answer them in pairs.

1 Bob / sleep?
2 Frank and Beth / sit on the sofa?
3 Frank / listen to music?
4 Beth / play a board game?
5 Kate / talk on the phone?

A: *Was Bob sleeping?*
B: *Yes, he was.*

Fun Spot

10 Go to page 106. Play *What were you doing yesterday at twelve o'clock?*

4.3 Grammar

I can use the Past Continuous and the Past Simple.
I can use adverbs of manner.

Doctor Q – Doctor Q's inventions

1 Look at the cartoon. Answer the questions.

1 Can you see any more of Doctor Q's inventions?
2 What do you think they do?

2 2.30 Listen and read. Complete the sentences.

1 Doctor Q invented the *cycle bubble* when he was twelve.
2 Pi is happy that he isn't ________ .
3 Doctor Q was studying when he ________ the snack maker.
4 Rob and Millie were outside when they heard a loud ________
5 Pi pushed the wrong ________ on the snack maker.

Grammar Past Continuous and Past Simple with *when*

I **was cycling** to school **when** it **started** to rain.
Rob and Millie **were working when** they **heard** a noise.

22 Get Grammar!

3 2.31 **Look at the pictures. Circle the correct answers. Then listen and check.**

1 Rob *watered* / *was watering* the plants when the storm *started* / *was starting*.
2 Doctor Q and Pi *made* / *were making* smoothies when the postman *arrived* / *was arriving*.
3 Millie *cleaned* / *was cleaning* when she *broke* / *was breaking* Doctor Q's favourite cup.
4 Pi *had* / *was having* a shower when the water *stopped* / *was stopping*.

4 Complete the sentences with the Past Continuous or the Past Simple form of the verbs. Who do you think is talking?

1 In the morning, Pi *was playing* (play) a game on the lab computer when I __________ (come) in!
2 Then, Millie and I __________ (work) in the lab when the lights __________ (go) out.
3 After lunch, Rob and I __________ (listen) to my favourite opera when the speakers __________ (break).
4 But in the evening, I __________ (paint) a picture when I __________ (have) a fantastic idea! What a day!

Grammar Adverbs of manner

patient ⟶ patient**ly** careful ⟶ careful**ly**
nice ⟶ nice**ly** easy ⟶ eas**ily**
good ⟶ **well** fast ⟶ **fast**

5 Which of these adverbs can you find in the cartoon?

6 2.32 **Complete the dialogue with adverbs of manner. Then listen and check.**

Dr Q: This is my first robot, Pi. It's very old. Turn it on [1] *carefully* (careful).
Robot: Hello! I'm CX-546.
Pi: I can't hear it. It's talking too [2] __________ (quiet).
Dr Q: How about now?
Robot: HELLO! I'M CX-546!!!
Pi: Now it's speaking too [3] __________ (loud)! CX-546 is very slow. Can't he walk [4] __________ (fast)?
Dr Q: No, but he knows how to make toast really [5] __________ (good). Here, try this!

Fun Spot

7 What were you doing when your friend took a silly photo of you? Use the words in the boxes to answer the question.

cycle dance sing talk walk

carefully happily loudly slowly badly

I was singing loudly when my friend took the photo.

I'm sorry to hear that!

Emma: You look upset. What's wrong?
Harry: I was writing my English essay last night when my laptop crashed!
Emma: Oh, I'm sorry to hear that! Does it work now?
Harry: No, it doesn't!
Emma: Oh, that's terrible! Can I help?
Harry: No, not really.
Emma: Why don't you take it to *Fast Fix* at the shopping centre? They can repair anything.
Harry: Good idea! Thanks.

A few days later …
Emma: Hi! What happened with your laptop?
Harry: Nothing. They can't repair it. It's too old.
Emma: That's a shame! Why do you look so happy then?
Harry: Because yesterday Mum and Dad bought a new one!
Emma: Lucky you!
Harry: Yeah!

1 23 2.33 **Watch or listen and read. Did they repair Harry's laptop at *Fast Fix*? How does he feel now? Why?**

2 2.34 **Listen and repeat.**

Communication Sympathising

Asking what happened

You look upset/worried.
What happened? / What's wrong?

Reacting to bad news

I'm sorry to hear that! / Oh, that's terrible! / That's a shame!

3 **Exam Spot** **Complete the dialogue with answers a–e. There are two extra answers.**

Uncle Joe: Hi, Poppy. You look worried. What's wrong?
Poppy: 1 ________
Uncle Joe: I'm sorry to hear that. Does it work now?
Poppy: 2 ________
Uncle Joe: Would you like to have my old phone?
Poppy: 3 ________
Uncle Joe: Now. I've got it with me.

a No, it doesn't. I went to *Fast Fix*, but they can't fix it.
b I was texting my friend when my mobile phone stopped working.
c I'm very upset.
d Wow! Thank you! When can I have it?
e Yes, please. *Fast Fix* can fix it too.

4 **Work in pairs. Act out dialogues. Use the ideas below and add your own.**

1 text my friend / drop my phone and break it
A: *You look upset.*
B: *I was texting my friend when I dropped my phone and broke it.*
A: *Oh, that's terrible!*
2 use my mum's tablet / crash
3 go to the cinema / miss the bus and be late
4 dry my hair / hairdryer stop working

The phone call that changed our world forever!

3rd April, 1973 was a cool spring day in New York City. People were walking in the street when they saw a man with a large object in his hands. He was holding it next to his ear and he was talking. But there was no one with him! Who was the man and who was he talking to?

The man was Martin Cooper and he worked for Motorola. He was talking to Joel S. Engel, who worked for a rival company. Engel was sitting at his desk when his phone rang. 'Joel, this is Marty,' said Martin. 'I'm calling you from a cell phone, a real hand-held portable cell phone*.' This was the first ever public mobile phone call.

The mobile phone Martin Cooper used was very different from smartphones today: It weighed 1.1 kg and it was 23 cm long. It only made phone calls. The battery lasted only twenty minutes.

Today, most smartphones weigh 100–200 grams. They have a touch screen, they can connect to Wi-Fi, you can talk for hours and charge them with a portable charger. There are apps for everything you want to do. You can even choose a different ringtone for each of your friends and family!

*__cell phone__ (American English) = **mobile phone** (British English)

1 I know that! Say what you can do with a smartphone that you can't do with a simple mobile phone. Use the verbs in the box and your own ideas.

chat download listen play surf take watch

I can chat online with my friends.

2 Exam Spot 2.35 Read and listen to the text. Choose the best title.

a The history of the telephone
b The first phone call from a smartphone
c The first public mobile phone call

3 Read the text again. Answer the questions.

1 Did the people in the street know what the man was holding next to his ear?
2 Where was Joel Engel when his phone rang?
3 Did Joel Engel and Martin Cooper work for the same company?
4 Was Martin's mobile phone heavier or lighter than a modern smartphone?
5 Did Martin's phone take photos?

4 2.36 Listen and repeat. Find these words in the text. Can you guess their meaning?

Vocabulary Smartphones

app battery portable charger
ringtone touch screen Wi-Fi

5 Complete the sentences with the words in the Vocabulary box.

1 I downloaded a useful *app*. Now I can add stickers to my photos.
2 Is there ________ in this place? I want to connect to the Internet.
3 Oh, no! My phone ________ is only 5%!
4 This song is very popular. Many people have it as a ________ on their phone!
5 He uses his phone all the time so he always carries a ________ charger with him.
6 The ________ of my phone is broken. Can you fix it for me?

Fun Spot

6 Work in groups. Play a speed game. Who is the fastest to:

1 name four things that run on batteries?
2 say four different things you can do with a phone app?
3 sing four different ringtones from your friends' and family mobiles?

4.6 Listening and Writing

I can understand and write a text about a past event.

1 Think about the last time when you felt happy, surprised, worried or silly. What happened? Tell your partner.

I made a silly mistake in a test. I was worried.

2 2.37 Listen to Neil and Meryl talking about what happened to them. Match the photos to the names. There are two extra photos.

A

B

C

D

E

F

G

H

1 Neil [*A*] [ ] [ ]   2 Meryl [ ] [ ] [ ]

3 2.37 Listen again. Circle T (true) or F (false).

1 It was Neil's Dad's birthday. T / (F)
2 Neil wanted to make pancakes. T / F
3 The noise of the blender woke Neil's mother. T / F
4 Meryl was surfing the Internet for fun when the lights went out. T / F
5 Meryl and her parents ate sandwiches that evening. T / F
6 Meryl enjoyed the evening with her parents. T / F

4 Did you like the stories? Which one did you like more?

5 Read Richard's story. How did he get home? Why do you think he felt silly and tired?

The wrong bus

1 Last week I was waiting for my bus at the bus stop. A lot of people were waiting too, but the buses were late.

2 In the end, a bus came and I got on. I sat down and took out my smartphone. I was watching a cat video when the bus stopped. I looked out of the window, but I was in the wrong part of town. I was on the wrong bus!

3 I didn't have any money to take another bus, so I walked home. I felt silly and tired but my brother thought it was funny!

6 Look at the Writing box. Does Richard follow these steps in his story?

Writing Using past tenses in a story

1 First, set the scene. Use the Past Continuous.
2 Then, describe the events. Use the Past Simple or the Past Continuous and the Past Simple with *when*.
3 Finally, describe the result and your feelings. Use the Past Simple.

7 Read the story again. Underline the Past Continuous and circle the Past Simple.

8 Writing Time Write a short story about a funny, interesting or silly thing that happened to you.

Find ideas

Make notes. Answer these questions to help you.
When and where did it happen?
What were you doing before it happened?
What were other people doing?
What was the main event?
What happened next?
How did you feel?

Draft

Write your story in three paragraphs.

Check and write

Check that you include all the information and that you use the Past Simple and Past Continuous correctly. Then write the final version of your story.

Vocabulary

1 Match 1–7 to a–g. Which of these items did you use yesterday?

1 [b] smart		a toothbrush
2 [ ] microwave		b TV
3 [ ] remote		c stick
4 [ ] electric		d oven
5 [ ] DVD		e player
6 [ ] USB		f control
7 [ ] games		g console

2 Complete the sentences with one word in each gap.

1 *Unplug* the lamp in the living room and take it upstairs.
2 Please ________ in the hairdryer for me. I want to dry my hair.
3 I turned ________ the TV and watched my favourite programme.
4 It's late. Turn ________ the lights and go to bed.

3 Read the sentences and write the words.

1 You can download this onto your smartphone. a*pp*
2 You can use it to connect to the Internet. W_-_ _
3 Your tablet doesn't need a mouse because it has this. t_ _ _ _ s_ _ _ _ _
4 This is inside your smartphone and laptop. You need to charge it. b_ _ _ _ _ _
5 You hear this when people phone your mobile phone. r_ _ _ _ _ _ _

Pronunciation

4 2.38 Listen and repeat: /ɜː/.

Two g**ir**ls were l**ear**ning new w**or**ds when they h**ear**d some singing b**ir**ds.

Grammar

5 Complete the sentences with the correct forms of the Past Continuous and the Past Simple.

1 It *was raining* (rain) when I *came* (come) out of the building.
2 Marty ________ (not brush) his teeth when the lights ________ (go) out.
3 The children ________ (study) when their mum ________ (ask) them to help her.
4 Julie ________ (walk) to school when she ________ (see) the accident.
5 We ________ (not have) dinner when Grandad ________ (call).
6 What ________ (you/do) when the postman ________ (arrive)?

6 Complete the sentences with the words in the box.

badly carefully easily fast ~~slowly~~ well

1 The old man was tired and he walked *slowly* .
2 The team won the match because they played ________ .
3 The road is dangerous, so don't drive ________ .
4 It wasn't a difficult exam, so I passed it ________ .
5 Don't break the dishes! Wash them ________ .
6 They did the work, but they did it ________ .

Communication

7 2.39 Complete the dialogues. Then listen and check.

happened shame terrible ~~What's~~ when

1 A: You don't look happy, Colin. [1] *What's* wrong?
B: I was having a shower [2] ________ the hot water ran out.
2 A: I can't come to the party tonight.
B: That's a [3] ________ !
3 A: You look worried. What [4] ________ ?
B: My cat is very ill.
A: That's [5] ________ !

Check yourself! ✓

- I can talk about useful objects powered by electricity. [ ]
- I can use the Past Simple and the Past Continuous. [ ]
- I can use adverbs of manner. [ ]
- I can express sympathy. [ ]

Reading and Writing

1 Exam Spot **Look at the picture and read the story. Complete the sentences about the story with one, two, three or four words.**

A weekend to remember

Two weeks ago, Helen went on an activity weekend with her class and two teachers, Mr Jones and Mrs Brown. They stayed in a small hostel called 'Mountainside Hostel'. It was near a big, beautiful mountain.
On Saturday, they wanted to explore the area, so Mr Jones said, 'Let's go hiking!' They had a great time and took a lot of photos. They walked a long way, so they got tired.

In the evening, they were very hungry. There wasn't a restaurant at the hostel, so the students cooked their dinner in the kitchen. It was nice and modern. There was a microwave oven, a blender and there were three toasters. At nine o'clock, Mrs Brown shouted, 'Bed time! There's a cycling trip tomorrow, so we must get up early.'

In the morning, it was very cold. Helen and her friends were getting ready when they heard shouting and laughing outside. 'What's happening?' Helen said to Jenny. They looked out of their bedroom window. Everything was white. It was snowy! Mr Jones was standing in the garden. 'We can't go cycling today', he said, 'but we can go to a restaurant for a nice hot meal!' They went to a very nice restaurant and tried the local food – it was delicious!

1 *Mountainside Hostel* was near a big, beautiful mountain.
2 The students and the teachers wanted ____________ on Saturday.
3 They ____________ because they walked a long way.
4 The boys and girls ____________ because the hostel didn't have a restaurant.
5 There were three ____________ in the hostel's kitchen.
6 They went to bed at nine o'clock because they wanted to go on ____________ on Sunday.
7 When the girls were getting ready they heard ____________ and laughing outside.
8 On Sunday they went to a restaurant and tried ____________ .

2 Exam Spot **Write 60–80 words about something that happened to you. Use these questions to help you.**

1 When did it happen? Describe the scene.
2 What were you doing before it happened and when it happened?
3 What happened next?
4 What was the result?
5 How did you feel?

Last summer I was in … with …
We were …
Later, I was … when …
I …
I felt …

Listening

3 Exam Spot 2.40 **Betty is talking to Tom. Listen and write the answers to questions 1–8.**

1 Where did Betty go yesterday? *Chester*
2 Who did she go with? ____________
3 Did she enjoy the trip? ____________
4 Was the weather good when they were driving to Chester? ____________
5 What happened to Betty's smartphone? ____________
6 Why did Betty and Sue go into a clothes shop? ____________
7 Was Betty's phone working? ____________
8 What was Betty doing when her parents walked into the café? ____________

Communication

4 **Exam Spot** **Complete the dialogue with answers a–h. There are two extra answers.**

Katy: You look upset Mum. What's wrong?
Mum: [1] *e*
Katy: That's a shame. Can I see it?
Mum: [2] ______
Katy: That's weird. I can't turn it on. When did you buy the phone?
Mum: [3] ______
Katy: Where did you buy it?
Mum: [4] ______
Katy: Where's your charger?
Mum: [5] ______
Katy: Can you plug the charger in and try to turn on the phone?
Mum: [6] ______

a The Wi-Fi wasn't very good.
b From *Smart Phone Store*! It was a special offer.
c Two weeks ago.
d It wasn't cheap.
e I was speaking to Dad when my smartphone stopped working.
f Yes, of course. Here it is.
g Yes, sure. Great! It's working now!
h In the kitchen. Just give me a minute.

5 **Exam Spot** **Ask and answer the questions in pairs.**

1 What did you do on your last holiday?
2 What holiday activities don't you like doing? Why?
3 What are your top three useful things from Unit 4? Why?
4 What were you doing when the English teacher walked into the classroom today?
5 What can you do well?

Exam Language Bank

Going on holiday
explore an area / a city / a town
go camping
go cycling
go hiking
go on a boat trip
go on a day trip
go on a guided tour
go snorkelling
go to the beach
try the local food

Phrases with *get*
get bored
get cold
get dark
get lost
get tired

Useful things
blender
DVD player
electric toothbrush
games console
hairdryer
microwave oven
remote control
smart TV
toaster
USB stick

Using technology
plug in
unplug
turn on
turn off

Smartphones
app
battery
portable charger
ringtone
touch screen
Wi-Fi

Requests
Making requests
Can you *bring me my phone*, please?
Could you give me *the key to my room*?
Can I *have the tablet*?
Responding to requests
Yes, no problem. / Yes, of course.
Sorry, *I/you* can't. *I'm using it right now.*
Not now, sorry. *I'm busy.*

Sympathising
Asking what happened
You look *upset/worried*.
What happened? / What's wrong?
Reacting to bad news
I'm sorry to hear that! / Oh, that's terrible. / That's a shame!

5 Health matters

Vocabulary I can talk about health problems.

In this unit

Vocabulary
- Health problems
- Injuries
- The body

Grammar
- *have to*
- *should*

24–25

5.2 Grammar video

26

5.2 Grammar animation

27

5.3 Grammar animation

28

5.4 Communication video

29

BBC Culture video

I know that!

1 **Complete the list of things that keep you healthy. How often do you do them?**

1 *wash* your hands
2 ______ some exercise
3 ______ fruit and vegetables
4 ______ to bed early
5 ______ a lot of water
6 ______ your teeth after a meal

2 Look at the picture on page 58 and read the captions. Who are the characters? What is wrong with them?

3 2.41 Listen and repeat. Which health problems do the superheroes have?

Vocabulary Health problems

Nouns

a blocked nose a cold a cough earache
a headache a runny nose a sore throat
a stomachache a temperature toothache

Verbs

cough sneeze

LOOK! *I've got / I have* a cough.
I'm coughing.

4 2.42 Listen to the superheroes. Match the names to characters A–F in the picture on page 58.

1 [F] Super Sue
2 [ ] Action Ann
3 [ ] Terrific Tom
4 [ ] Wonder Wendy
5 [ ] Fantastic Frank
6 [ ] Mega Max

5 Label the photos with the words in the Vocabulary box.

1 She's got *earache*.

2 She's got __________.

3 He's got __________.

4 He's got __________.

6 Work in pairs. Student A: Mime an illness. Student B: Guess what's wrong with A.

B: *You've got a temperature.*
A: *No, I haven't.*
B: *You've got a headache.*
A: *That's right.*

7 Which of the problems in the Vocabulary box do you have when you have a cold?

8 Complete the dialogues. Use the Vocabulary box to help you.

1
Do your homework now, Jules.
I can't think, Dad. I've got a terrible *headache*.

2
It's lunchtime, everyone!
I don't want lunch, Mum. I ate too many crisps and now I have a ________.

3
I feel terrible.
Your head is hot. I think you've got a ________.

4
Can I stay at home today, Mum? I'm coughing and I've got a runny nose.
Hmm. You have a bad ________. OK. Go to bed!

5
I have a ________ throat, doctor.
Open your mouth … Yes, of course you do. Your throat is red.

I remember that!

9 Draw a person who has two or more health problems at the same time.

10 Present your picture to the class. Ask them to guess what health problems it presents.
He has a runny nose and a temperature.

5.2 **Grammar** I can use the verb *have to.*

She has to stay in bed

Emma: OK … Get well soon! Bye!
Gran: Who's ill?
Emma: Poppy. She's got the flu. She has to stay in bed. At least she doesn't have to study for the French test.
Gran: Poor girl! Well, we all have to be careful, Emma. It's easy to catch the flu at this time of the year.

Emma: Oh, no!
Gran: What's the matter, darling?
Emma: Poppy's got my new dance shoes! I put them in her bag when we went shopping. I have to go and get them.
Gran: You don't have to wear your new shoes. You've got your old ones.
Emma: My old shoes are too small, Gran.

Gran: Do you really have to go there when Poppy's got the flu?
Emma: Yes, I do. Don't worry, Gran. I don't have to go near Poppy. I'm not even going to go into her room.
Gran: Hmm.
Emma: Poppy? It's me again! Can I come and pick up my shoes before I go to my dance class? … OK, see you soon!

A few days later …

1 ▶ 24 🔊 **2.43** **Watch or listen and read. Why is Gran worried?**

2 **Circle the correct answer.**

1 Poppy is staying at home today because she *isn't well* / *wants to study for a test.*
2 Emma's shoes are *in her shopping bag* / *at Poppy's house.*
3 Emma can't wear her other shoes because they *are the wrong size* / *look too old.*
4 Emma isn't going to go inside Poppy's *house* / *room.*
5 Emma is going to *Poppy's house* / *her dance class* first.

3 🔊 **2.44** **Listen and repeat. Find these expressions in the story.**

Say it!

Get well soon! It's me again! See you soon!

4 ▶ **Guess!** **Who is the person on the sofa? Have a class vote.**

a Poppy **b** Emma **c** Gran

5 ▶ 25 🔊 **2.45** **Now watch or listen and check.**

Grammar *have to*

26 Get Grammar!

+	−
I/You/We/They **have to** go.	I/You/We/They **don't have to** go.
He/She/It **has to** go.	He/She/It **doesn't have to** go.
?	**Short answers**
Do I/you/we/they **have to** go?	Yes, I/you/we/they **do**. No, I/you/we/they **don't**.
Does he/she/it **have to** go?	Yes, he/she/it **does**. No, he/she/it **doesn't**.

How long **does** she **have to** stay in bed?

You **have to** do it. = It's necessary.
You **don't have to** do it. = It's not necessary.

6 Complete the sentences with the correct form of *have to*.

1 Gran's got the flu. She *has to* see a doctor. ✔
2 Emma ____________ do the shopping because Gran can't go out. ✔
3 Poppy is well now. She ____________ stay in bed. ✘
4 George and Harry's mum is ill. They ____________ be quiet at home. ✔
5 Mum ____________ go outside to see the doctor – Dad can help her! ✘
6 George and Harry ____________ study for an important test this week. ✔

7 Complete Harry's blog post with the words in the box.

~~do~~ doesn't don't don't has have have to

What [1] *do* you to have to do?

I [2] ________ to practise tennis on Tuesdays, Thursdays and at the weekend. The sports centre is near so I [3] ________ have to get up early. It's only a five-minute walk.

George doesn't play tennis, so he [4] ________ have to go to the practice. But he [5] ________ to do a lot of other things. He's always very busy.

When we go out with our friends, we have [6] ________ tell our parents where we are. We [7] ________ have to be back home early, but we [8] ________ to answer the phone!

8 Work in pairs. Ask and answer the questions.

1 what time / be in bed on weekdays?
2 get up early on Mondays?
3 do homework before dinner?
4 help your family with the housework?
5 what time / be back home on Saturdays?
6 tell your parents where you are after school?
7 play basketball at school?

A: *What time do you have to be in bed on weekdays?*
B: *I have to be in bed at 9 p.m.*
A: *Do you have to get up early on Mondays?*
B: *No, I don't.*

9 Tell the class about your partner.

Marisa has to be in bed at nine o'clock on weekdays. She doesn't have to get up early on Mondays.

Fun Spot

10 Write your own crazy school or house rules for a day!

You have to eat chocolate for breakfast.
You don't have to eat salad today!

Doctor Q The camping trip

1 **Look at the cartoon. How many different wild animals can you see? Point to them and say the names.**

2 2.46 **Listen and read. Circle T (true) or F (false).**

1 It's warm and sunny. T / F
2 Rob pushed the button too early. T / F
3 It wasn't a good night for Doctor Q. T / F
4 There was a mosquito net in the tent. T / F
5 At first, Doctor Q doesn't believe that there is a bear. T / F

Grammar *should*

+	I/He/She/It **should** lie down. We/You/They **should** lie down.	
–	I/He/She/It **shouldn't** lie down. We/You/They **shouldn't** lie down.	
?	**Should** I/he/she/it lie down?	Yes, I/he/she/it **should**. No, I/he/she/it **shouldn't**.
	Should we/you/they lie down?	Yes, we/you/they **should**. No, we/you/they **shouldn't**.
	What **should** we do?	

27 Get Grammar!

Fluffy ***should*** *exercise more. She* ***shouldn't*** *sleep on the sofa all day.*

3 Match pictures A–F to sentences 1–6.

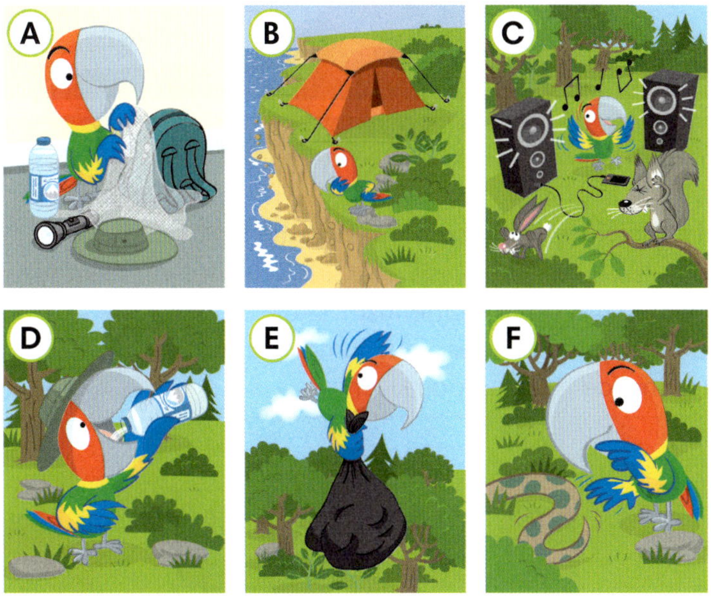

1 [D] You should drink a lot of water.
2 [ ] You should take a mosquito net.
3 [ ] You shouldn't leave any rubbish.
4 [ ] You shouldn't touch wild animals.
5 [ ] You shouldn't make a lot of noise.
6 [ ] You should put up your tent in a safe place.

4 Complete the sentences with *should* or *shouldn't*.

1 It's a very hot and sunny day. Doctor Q wants to go sightseeing in the city tomorrow.
  a He *should* wear a hat and sunglasses.
  b He ________ stay in the sun for long.
  c He ________ take a map.
2 Millie and Rob are going to stay at home.
  a They ________ look after Pi.
  b They ________ open the door to anyone.
  c They ________ clean the house.

5 I know that! How many parts of the body can you name?

6 2.47 Listen and repeat. Look at the picture and complete the text with the words in the Vocabulary box.

Vocabulary Injuries

broken leg   bruise   burn   cut
mosquito bite

Doctor Q has got a 1 *burn* and a 2 ________ on his arm, lots of 3 ________ bites all over his body and a 4 ________ on his head. He's also got a 5 ________ leg. Poor Doctor Q!

Fun Spot

7 Exam Spot Work in pairs. Ask and answer questions.
Student A: Go to page 106.
Student B: Go to page 112.

You should lie down

Mum: You don't look well, sweetheart.
Harry: I feel terrible. I've got a headache.
Mum: I think you should lie down.
Harry: Yes, that's a good idea.
George: Mum, I don't feel very well.
Mum: Oh, no! You too? What's the matter?
George: I've got … erm … a stomachache. What should I do?
Mum: Why don't you drink some mint tea? It's good for your stomach.
George: Yes, you're right. Oh, a text from David. Yes! David says that tomorrow's History test is off.
Mum: George?
George: You know, Mum? I suddenly feel a lot better. Nice biscuits!

1 ▶ 28 🔊 2.48 **Watch or listen and read. What's wrong with Harry? Is George really ill?**

2 🔊 2.49 **Listen and repeat.**

Communication
Giving health advice

Asking about health
What's the matter? / What's wrong?

Responding
I don't feel very well. / I feel terrible.
I've got a *headache/cut*.

Giving advice
Why don't you *lie down* / *take a painkiller* / *drink some mint tea*?
Put *some cream* / *some ice* / *a plaster* on it.
I think you should see the *doctor/dentist*.

Accepting advice
Yes, that's a good idea. / Yes, you're right.

3 Label the pictures with the phrases in the box.

drink mint tea	see the dentist	see the doctor	lie down	~~put a plaster~~	put some cream	put some ice	take a painkiller

a  *put a plaster*
b 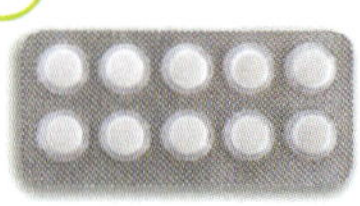 ____________
c  ____________
d  ____________
e  ____________
f  ____________
g  ____________
h 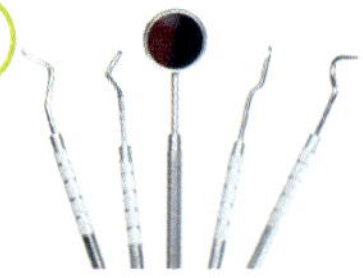 ____________

4 🔊 2.50 **Match the phrases in Exercise 3 to 1–4. You can use the phrases more than once. Then listen and check.**

1 a cut [*a*]
2 a headache [ ] [ ]
3 a bruise [ ] [ ]
4 toothache [ ] [ ]

5 Work in pairs. Take turns to give advice for the problems in Exercise 4. Use the Communication box to help you.

A: *What's the matter?*
B: *I've got a cut on my finger.*
A: *You should put a plaster on it.*

Do you want to feel better? Exercise!

Exercise is good for you, but what exactly does it do to your body? Let's find out!

The heart does more work than any other muscle in your body. It beats about 100,000 times a day! When you exercise, it beats faster because it has to send more blood to your muscles. This makes your heart stronger and you get fitter – you don't get tired quickly and you have energy. Your muscles get bigger and stronger. You can move, run and carry heavy things more easily.

What about the rest of your body?

When you exercise, your heart sends more blood to your brain too. You learn more quickly, you feel more relaxed and happier, and you sleep better.

Exercise is also important for your bones. Young people have strong bones, but when you get older, your bones become weaker. There are 206 bones in your body (52 are in your feet and 54 in your hands), and you have to exercise to keep them strong.

REMEMBER: People who exercise don't get ill as often as people who don't exercise. And you don't have to go to a gym to exercise. Just stay active!

Here's what you should do:

- **Do a sport – it's fun!**
- **Dance – with your friends or on your own!**
- **Ride your bike or walk – sometimes it's faster than the car or the bus!**

1 Work in pairs. Why do people exercise?

2 2.51 Listen and repeat. Then label pictures 1–5 with the words in the Vocabulary box.

Vocabulary The body

blood bones brain heart muscles

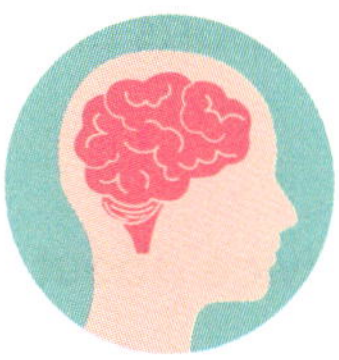

1 *brain*

2 ______

3 ______

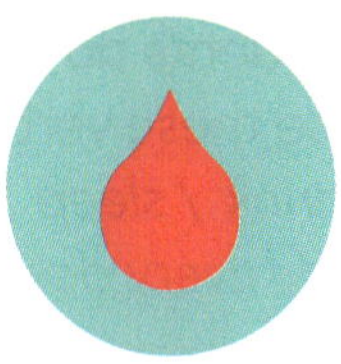

4 ______

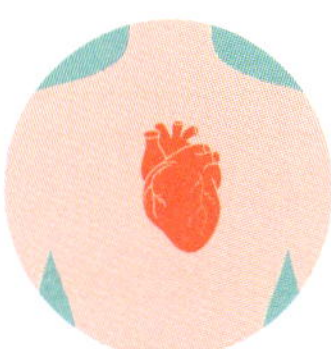

5 ______

3 2.52 Read and listen to the text. Underline the words from the Vocabulary box.

4 Read the text again. Answer the questions.

1 Which is the hardest-working muscle in your body?
2 Why does your heart beat faster when you exercise?
3 Why is exercise good for your brain?
4 What happens to your bones when you get older?
5 How many bones are there in your body?
6 How many bones are there in your feet?

5 2.53 Listen to three children. What kinds of exercise do they do? Write.

1 *dancing* 2 ______ 3 ______

6 Ask four of your classmates and find out what kinds of exercise they do.

Name	Exercise
1 ______	
2 ______	
3 ______	
4 ______	

What kind of exercise do you do?

7 Tell the class about your classmates.

Thomas doesn't do exercise at all, but Marta walks to school every day. She also likes dancing.

5.6 Listening and Writing

I can understand and write texts giving advice.

1 What should you do to get ready for an important test or sports competition? Write T (test), C (competition) or B (both).

- ☐ study every day
- ☐ leave home early to be on time
- ☐ have a good breakfast on the day
- ☐ go to bed early on the day before
- ☐ practise a bit every day

2 2.54 Listen to an interview. What is it about? Listen and tick (✔).

A ☐

B ☐

C ☐

3 Exam Spot 2.54 Listen again and complete.

1 Steve Roberts: basketball *coach*
2 Practise: ________ times a week
3 Good snack before game: some ________
4 In a match: players have to think and move ________
5 Before a match: do a warm-up to get your ________ ready
6 To win: you have to stay ________

4 What do you think players should do after an important match?

5 Read the magazine text. What is a charity walk?

Get ready to walk for charity!

Do you want to collect money for sick children? Take part in the charity walk next term! It's ten kilometres. It isn't easy so you have to get fit!

You should walk for thirty minutes three days a week. Walk a bit longer every week, but you don't have to walk every day. You should also go swimming and cycling to help your muscles get strong. Eat healthy food for energy and don't forget: you have to take water with you when you go for long walks. You should sleep for eight hours a day. Sleep is important for your body and your mind.

6 Read the Writing box. Underline the structures for giving advice in the text in Exercise 5.

Writing Structures for giving advice

We can give instructions or advice in different ways.

Walk a bit longer every week, but you don't have to walk every day.

You should walk for thirty minutes three days a week.

You have to get fit!

7 Rewrite the sentences. Use the words in brackets.

1 You shouldn't forget to do a good warm-up. (DON'T)
Don't forget to do a good warm-up.
2 Start preparing a few months before the walk. (HAVE TO)
3 It's a good idea to practise with a friend. (SHOULD)
4 It's not necessary for you to buy special sports clothes. (NOT HAVE TO)

8 Writing Time Write a text to give advice about how to do well in a test.

Find ideas
What should students do to do well in a test? Make notes. Use these verbs.
study / eat / drink / sleep
You should study every day.

Draft
Write your text.

Check and write
Make sure you use different structures to give instructions or advice. Then write the final version of your text.

Vocabulary

1 Look at the picture and complete the health problems 1–6.

1 a *runny* nose
2 ________
3 a ________ throat
4 a ________
5 a ________
6 a ________ leg

2 Complete the words.

1 Josh goes to the gym to make his **m***uscles* stronger.
2 You use your **b**________ to think.
3 Your **h**________ beats faster when you exercise.
4 The red liquid in your body is called **b**________.
5 Cheese and milk make your **b**________ strong.

Grammar

3 Complete the email with the correct form of *have to* and the verbs in brackets.

Hi Vanessa,
I can't come to the beach with you. Mum and Dad are having a party and we [1] *have to get* (get) the house ready. There's a lot to do!
Dad [2] ____________ (tidy) the garden, Mum [3] ____________ (prepare) the food and I [4] ____________ (help) them. My little brothers [5] ____________ (not do) any chores.
What about you? Are you doing anything nice this morning or [6] ____________ (you / do) chores?
See you soon.
Cassandra

4 Look at the problems and give advice. Use the verbs in the box and *should/shouldn't*.

leave home without breakfast
~~ask your teacher for help~~ go to the vet
practise every day use your mobile in bed

1 I don't understand my homework.
You should ask your teacher for help.
2 I can't sleep at night.
3 My brother really wants to win a match.
4 My gran's dog is ill.
5 My friend gets very hungry before lunch.

Pronunciation

5 2.55 Listen and repeat: /eɪ/ or /əʊ/.

I've got a headache, a sore throat,
my nose is very red.
I have to take painkillers,
I have to stay in bed.

Communication

6 2.56 Circle the correct answer. Then listen and check.

1 **A:** You don't look [1]*ill / well*.
B: I've got a headache.
A: Why [2]*aren't / don't* you lie down and take a [3]*painkiller / plaster*?
2 **A:** What's the [4]*matter / wrong*?
B: I've got mosquito [5]*break / bites* all over my body!
A: You should put some [6]*mint tea / cream* on them.
B: Good idea.

Check yourself!

- I can talk about health problems and injuries. ☐
- I can use *have to* and *should*. ☐
- I can give health advice. ☐

Get Culture! British TV

Sir David Attenborough

If you watch TV, you probably know Sir David Attenborough's work. After all, he is the 'godfather' of wildlife documentaries and one of the most loved and respected people in Britain.

His love of nature started when he was just a boy. He was interested in fossils and he had a big collection of them. It was no surprise that he decided to study Natural Sciences at Cambridge University.

When he began his career at the BBC, in 1952, there weren't many programmes about nature. Sir David changed that with a series of documentaries called *Zoo Quest*. For the first time, film crews travelled all over the world and brought back black and white films showing animals in their natural environment. Sir David produced a lot more wildlife documentaries after that. They were all very popular. *Life on Earth* had millions of viewers worldwide.

A FOSSIL

His work still inspires viewers of all ages, all over the world. The films are now in full colour, HD and even 3D. With the help of technology, we can see the world through the eyes of a bird flying high in the sky, a fish swimming deep in the ocean or a very small insect on a tree.

A number of plants, insects and birds have Sir David's name. That's a great way to say a big 'thank you' to the man who spends so much of his time caring for nature and protecting it.

FILMING FISH IN THE OCEAN

1 **Look at the photos. Do you know the man talking to the camera? What are his programmes about?**

2 **2.57 Read and listen to the text. Circle T (true) or F (false).**

1. Sir David Attenborough is very popular in the UK. (T) / F
2. Before Sir David started his work for the BBC, they had no programmes about nature at all. T / F
3. Sir David's first TV series was called *Zoo Quest*. T / F
4. You can watch Sir David's work only on UK TV. T / F
5. Sir David doesn't use new technology to film his documentaries. T / F

3 **Look at the types of TV programmes. Can you give examples of each type of programme?**

cartoon (science/wildlife) documentary game show news sitcom soap opera talent show

4 **2.58 Listen to an interview with two young people about TV programmes. Answer the questions.**

1. What kind of documentaries does Ashley like?
2. Who watches documentaries with Ashley?
3. What sitcoms does Ashley like?
4. What kind of programme does Ashley's mother prefer?
5. What sport does Jake like watching on TV?
6. What do Jake's parents like watching on TV?

5 **Do you like watching wildlife documentaries? Why? / Why not?**

BBC

A ▶29 **Watch the video clip and answer the presenter's questions. Which programme is the BBC very well-known for?**

B ▶29 **Watch the video again. Complete the sentences.**

1 In the beginning, the BBC only broadcast ________ programmes.
2 The BBC TV service started in ________ .
3 ________ million people watched the Queen's coronation in ________ .
4 About ________ thousand people work for the BBC.
5 There are ________ BBC TV channels in the UK and ________ international channels.

C **How many TV channels are there in your country? Vote for the top three as a class.**

PROJECT

- **Work in groups of 8–10. What types of TV programmes can you watch on TV in your country? Look at the box in Exercise 3 to help you.**
- **Do a survey about the TV programmes the people in your group watch. Use these questions to help.**

  What are your favourite types of programmes?
  Why do you like them?
  What types of programmes don't you like?
  Why don't you like them?

- **Make a digital presentation about your findings. Add photos for each part of your presentation.**

- **Show your presentation to the class. What is the most popular type of programme?**

6 Cooking and eating

Vocabulary I can talk about cooking.

In this unit

Vocabulary
- Cooking verbs
- Cooking nouns
- Serving and eating food
- Describing food

Grammar
- Present Perfect affirmative and negative
- Present Perfect questions, *ever* and *never*

30-31 6.2 Grammar video

32 6.2 Grammar animation

33 6.3 Grammar animation

34 6.4 Communication video

I know that!

1 How many words can you add to each group? Compare in pairs.

1 Vegetables: *carrots, …*
2 Fruit: *apples, …*
3 Milk products
4 Meat

Cooking for beginners

Cooking for beginners

Anyone can learn to make their favourite dishes. Why don't you take our online cooking course and see? These photos show you some cooking basics.

1

2

3

4

5

6

7

8

9

10

⚠ Make sure there's an adult in the house when you use the oven, boil or fry food.

2 3.1 Read and listen to the text on page 70. What can you learn on the online course?

3 3.2 Listen and repeat. Look at the photos on page 70. Complete the photo labels below with the cooking verbs.

Vocabulary Cooking verbs

add bake beat boil chop fry mix peel roast slice

Photo 1: *chop* the onions and garlic
Photo 2: ______ the eggs
Photo 3: ______ the potatoes
Photo 4: ______ the vegetables
Photo 5: ______ the cocoa with the eggs and butter
Photo 6: ______ the vegetables
Photo 7: ______ the pasta
Photo 8: ______ the potatoes in hot oil
Photo 9: ______ the cake at 160°C
Photo 10: ______ some salt

LOOK!

You **bake** bread, a cake and biscuits.
You **roast** meat, chicken and vegetables.

4 Match the activities in Exercise 3 to the dishes below. There is one extra activity.

Roasted vegetables [*1*] [ ] [ ]
Chips [ ] [ ] [ ]
Chocolate cake [ ] [ ] [ ]

5 3.3 Listen and repeat. Find the objects on page 70.

Vocabulary Cooking nouns

bowl cake tin frying pan oven pot

bowl – photos 2 and 5

6 Read and circle the correct words.

Here are three simple recipes for you to try:

Simple fruit salad

[1]*Peel / Boil* and slice some apples. Then put them in a [2]*oven / bowl* with some strawberries and orange juice. [3]*Beat / Mix* to make a simple – and healthy – fruit salad!

Simple cake

Mix 125 grams of butter with 125 grams of sugar. Then [4]*chop / add* two eggs and 125 grams of flour. Bake the cake in the [5]*pot / oven* for 20 minutes. When it is cool, take it out of the [6]*frying pan / cake tin*.

Simple chicken legs

[7]*Fry / Mix* some oil, lemon juice, salt and pepper in a bowl. Put the chicken legs in the bowl and leave them for two hours. [8]*Boil / Roast* the chicken legs in the oven for about 35 minutes.

7 3.4 Listen and circle the correct answer.

1 What fruit is Tom using for the dessert?
a apples (b) bananas c oranges
2 Where is he putting the fruit?
a in a bowl b in a pot c in a cake tin
3 What isn't he using for the sauce?
a orange juice b butter c sugar
4 What is Tom doing next?
a frying the dessert b baking the dessert
c roasting the dessert

I remember that!

8 How many words can you remember? Compare with a partner.

1 Ways to cook food:
boil, …
2 Ways to prepare vegetables for cooking
3 Things you use to cook food

6.2 Grammar

I can use the Present Perfect in affirmative and negative sentences.

We've brought dessert!

Gran Bertie and Emma are cooking Sunday lunch for the family.

1

Emma: I've chopped the cucumber, Gran. What's next?
Gran: Let's have a look. OK. 'Put some olive oil and lemon juice in a small bowl and mix them with a spoon.'
Emma: All the small bowls are in the dishwasher. It hasn't finished. How about this mug?
Gran: Yes, that's fine.

2

Harry: Hi, Gran! Hi, Emma!
George: We've brought dessert!
Emma: Oh, good! Gran hasn't made dessert today!
Gran: Yes, I have. I've baked apples.
Emma: Apples are fruit, Gran. Not dessert!

3

George: What's for lunch?
Gran: We've made chicken pie, chips and salad.
George: Good! I'm starving!
Gran: George, Harry, can you set the table, please? I've taken out the knives and forks. They're over there. The plates are in the cupboard. Emma, put the chips on the table.
Emma: Erm … Gran?

1 30 3.5 **Watch or listen and read. What are Gran, Emma and the the boys going to eat for lunch?**

2 Read the story. Complete the sentences with one word.

1 Today it is *Sunday*.
2 There aren't any clean ________.
3 Emma doesn't like ________ for dessert.
4 ________ is very hungry.
5 There are no plates on the ________ yet.

3 3.6 **Listen and repeat. Find the expressions in the story.**

Say it!

What's next? Let's have a look.
I'm starving!

4 Guess! **Why is Emma surprised? Make a guess.**

5 31 3.7 **Now watch or listen and check.**

Grammar Present Perfect affirmative and negative

▶ 32 Get Grammar!

+	−
Regular verbs	
I/You/We/They've baked apples.	I/You/We/They haven't baked apples.
He/She/It's baked apples.	He/She/It hasn't baked apples.
Irregular verbs	
I/You/We/They've eaten the chips.	I/You/We/They haven't eaten the chips.
He/She/It's eaten the chips.	He/She/It hasn't eaten the chips.

've = have 's = has haven't = have not hasn't = has not

6 In your notebook, write the Past Simple and the Present Perfect form of the verbs. For irregular verbs, look at page 111.

~~bake~~ ~~break~~ bring buy chop drink eat have hear leave make put tidy wash

Regular verbs	Irregular verbs
bake – baked – baked	*break – broke – broken*

7 Complete the sentences with the Present Perfect form of the verbs.

1 **Emma:** We *have made* (make) lunch and we ___ (tidy) the living room.
2 **Gran:** I ___ (wash) the vegetables and Emma ___ (chop) them.
3 **Harry:** Our parents ___ (buy) a cake and we ___ (set) the table.
4 **George:** Harry ___ (eat) almost all the chips!

8 Complete Emma's texts messages to Poppy.

not add not try not leave ~~not have~~ not put

Harry and George [1] *haven't had* breakfast so they're hungry. I hope they like our lunch! 13:02

We [2] ___ the cola in the fridge so it isn't cold enough to drink! 13:10

Gran [3] ___ any salt to the pie and it's not good. I [4] ___ the cake because George [5] ___ any for me. 13:12

13:14 Oh, no!

9 🔊 3.8 Listen and repeat. Find these items in the picture of Nell's kitchen below.

Vocabulary
Serving and eating food

cup fork glass knife mug plate spoon

10 🔊 3.9 Look at the picture. What has or hasn't Nell done? Use the words in the box to make sentences. Listen and check.

~~break the cup~~ eat the apple use the plate wash the mug drink the water slice the bread make tea eat the cake

She has broken the cup.

11 Close your books. Take turns to tell your partner the sentences from Exercise 10.

6.3 Grammar I can ask questions using the Present Perfect.

Doctor Q The popcorn

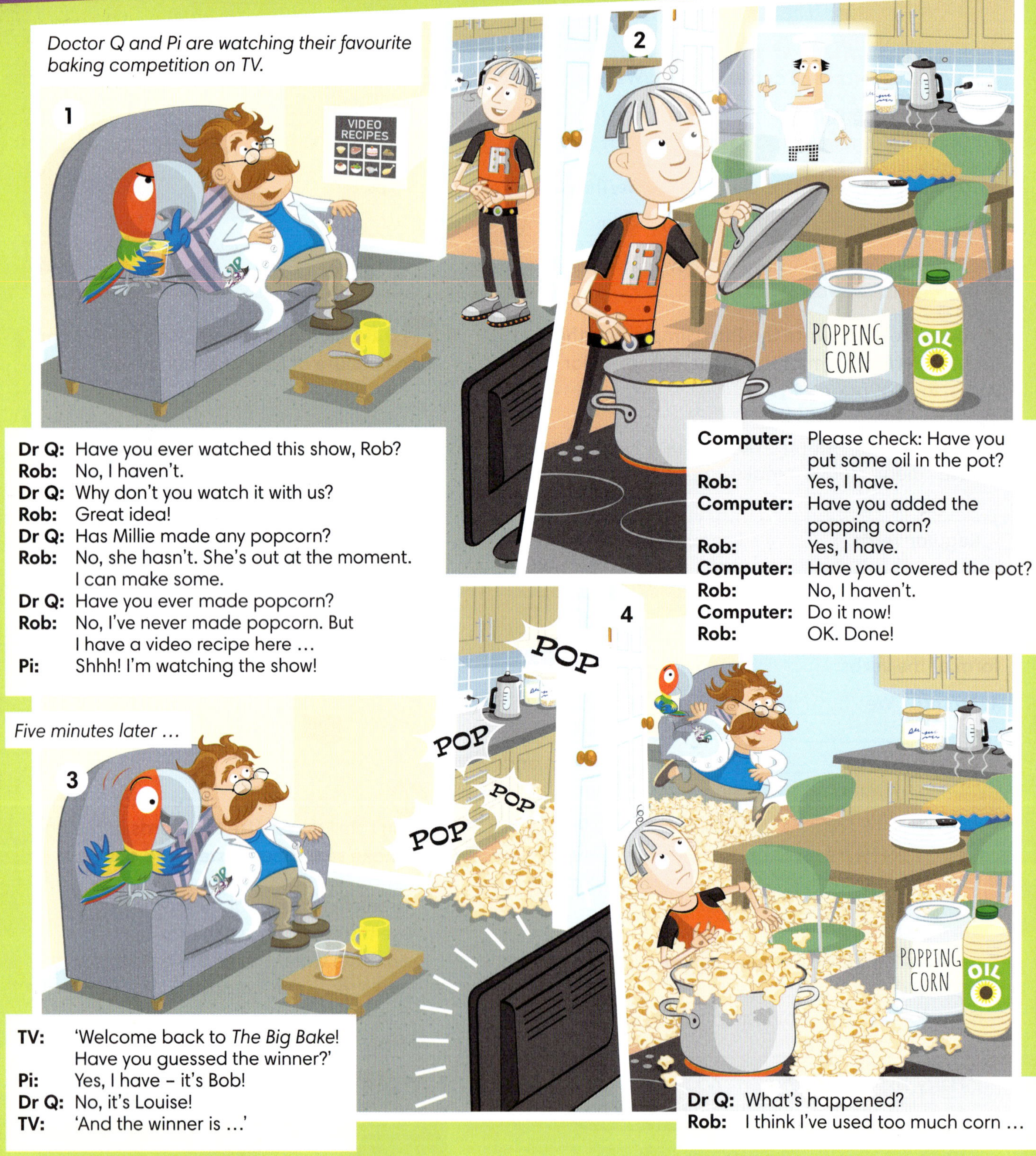

1 Look at the cartoon. How many objects for cooking and eating can you find?

bowl cup fork glass knife
mug plate pot spoon

2 3.10 Listen and read. Answer the questions.

1. What are Doctor Q and Pi doing?
2. Is Millie at home?
3. What ingredients does Rob use to make popcorn?
4. What's the name of Doctor Q and Pi's favourite TV show?

Grammar
Present Perfect questions, *ever* and *never*

Regular and irregular verbs	
?	Short answers
Have I/you/we/they started? Have I/you/we/they won?	Yes, I/you/we/they have. No, I/you/we/they haven't.
Has he/she/it started? Has he/she/it won?	Yes, he/she/it has. No, he/she/it hasn't.
What has he done?	
ever, never	
Have you ever made popcorn? No, I haven't. I've never made popcorn.	

33 Get Grammar!

3 Complete the questions about the cartoon.

Picture 1

1 *Has* Doctor Q *taken off* his lab coat? (take off)
2 ________ the show ________ ? (start)

Picture 2

3 ________ Millie ________ a pie for dinner? (make)
4 ________ Rob ________ all the corn? (use)

Picture 3

5 ________ Pi ________ his juice? (drink)
6 ________ Doctor Q and Pi ________ the name of the winner? (hear)

4 Work in pairs. Ask and answer the questions in Exercise 3.

A: *Has Doctor Q taken off his lab coat?*
B: *No, he hasn't.*

5 Doctor Q wants to be in *The Big Bake* TV show. Write the interviewer's questions.

1 ever / be on TV?
Have you ever been on TV? ✗
2 ever / take part in a cooking competition?
________ ☐
3 ever / bake a cake?
________ ☐
4 ever / make ice cream?
________ ☐
5 ever / try chocolate biscuits with chilli?
________ ☐

6 3.11 Listen to the interview. Write a tick (✓) or a cross (✗) next to the questions in Exercise 5.

7 Interview your partner. Use the questions in Exercise 5.

A: *Have you ever been on TV?* B: *Yes, I have!*

8 Match the questions to answers in each pair.

1 *b* Have you ever eaten pesto?
2 ☐ Have you eaten all the pesto?
a Yes, I have. Sorry!
b No, I haven't. What is pesto?

3 ☐ Has he ever won a competition?
4 ☐ Has he won the competition?
a Yes, he has. It was a talent show last year.
b Yes, he has. He's the fastest runner today.

5 ☐ Have they cooked dinner?
6 ☐ Have they ever cooked dinner before?
a Yes, they have and it smells lovely!
b No, it's the first time they've cooked dinner.

Fun Spot

9 Make a class survey. What have your classmates never done? Use the expressions in the box and your own ideas.

make popcorn	stay at a hotel
visit London	win a singing competition

A: *Have you ever won a singing competition?*
B: *No, I haven't.*
A: *Jim has never won a singing competion.*

I'd prefer cheese

Poppy: It's sunny today! Let's go out somewhere.
Emma: Good idea. Would you like to have a picnic or go for a bike ride?
Poppy: I'd really like to go for a bike ride.
Emma: OK. You know what? We can have a picnic in the park too!
Poppy: Let's do that! Mum's made her special lemonade. I can bring some.
Emma: And I can make sandwiches. Would you like cheese or tuna?
Poppy: I'd prefer cheese.
Emma: OK. How about something sweet? Would you like chocolate cake or biscuits?
Poppy: Hmm … You choose.
Emma: Chocolate biscuits!
Poppy: Brilliant! See you in fifteen minutes!

Emma: Bye, Gran! … Oh, no! I don't believe it!

1 34 3.12 **Watch or listen and read. What do Poppy and Emma decide to do? Why can't they do it?**

2 3.13 **Listen and repeat.**

Communication Preferences

Asking about preferences
Would you like to *have a picnic* or *go for a bike ride*?
Would you like *cheese* or *tuna*?

Responding
I'd like to *go for a bike ride*.
I'd like *cheese*. / I'd prefer *cheese*.
You choose. / I don't mind.

3 3.14 **Complete the dialogue with the words in the box. Then listen and check.**

choose I'd mind or prefer to ~~Would~~

Philip: I'm thirsty. Can I have a drink?
Mickey: Sure. [1]*Would* you like juice or water?
Philip: [2]________ like some water, please.
Alice: I'd [3]________ some juice, Mickey.
Mickey: Now, would you like [4]________ watch a DVD [5]________ play a game?
Philip: I don't [6]________.
Alice: You [7]________.
Mickey: OK. Let's watch a DVD, then.

4 Exam Spot 3.15 **Listen and tick (✔) the correct answer a, b or c.**

1 Where are the family going to go on holiday?

a ☐  b ☐  c ☐ 

2 What month are they going to travel?

a ☐ 

b ☐ 

c ☐ 

3 How are they going to travel?

a ☐  b ☐  c ☐ 

5 **In pairs, ask and answer about your preferences.**

1 For lunch today: sandwiches or pizza?
A: *Would you like sandwiches or pizza for lunch today?*
B: *I'd prefer sandwiches.*

2 To do on Saturday morning: go shopping or go cycling?
B: *Would you like to go shopping or go cycling on Saturday morning?*
A: *I'd like to go cycling.*

6 **Go to page 106. Act out dialogues.**

WOULD YOU LIKE KETCHUP WITH YOUR ICE CREAM?

1 ☐ Ice cream is nothing new. The Chinese ate ice cream two thousand years ago. They mixed milk and rice and froze it in snow. The ancient Romans loved eating snow with honey and fruit. For many years, ice cream was only for rich people. The ingredients were expensive and it cost a lot to keep it cold. Today ice cream is for everyone!

2 ☐ Have you ever tried to make ice cream? It's simple. All you need is milk or cream and sugar. Some recipes use eggs too. Then you can add vanilla (the most popular flavour), chocolate, strawberries or other ingredients. If you only have fruit and sugar, you can make a delicious sorbet. A sweet and sour lemon sorbet is great in the summer.

3 ☐ If you are not afraid to try, there are some unusual ice cream flavours too. Have you ever eaten spicy ice cream with chocolate and chilli? You can also make ice cream with salty biscuits in it. What about these flavours? There's sausage ice cream and cheese ice cream. There's even black ice cream with charcoal in it. Check out the photo!

Comments:

molly15: I've seen charcoal ice cream, but I haven't tried it because it sounds disgusting.

Ice Age: I've had charcoal ice cream and it wasn't too bad.

I-scream!: I love chocolate ice cream, but I've never had it with chilli! I'm going to try it!

1 Do you like ice cream? What's your favourite flavour?

2 🔊 3.16 Listen and read. Match headings a–d to paragraphs 1–3. There is one extra heading.

a Is ice cream good for you?
b More interesting than vanilla or chocolate?
c What do you need to make ice cream?
d How old is ice cream?

3 Read the blog again. Answer the questions.

1 What did the Chinese use to make ice cream?
2 Why was ice cream expensive in the past?
3 What is the most popular ice cream flavour?
4 What can you use to make ice cream spicy?
5 What does black ice cream have in it?
6 Has molly15 ever eaten charcoal ice cream?

4 🔊 3.17 Listen and repeat. Then find the words in the text.

Vocabulary Describing food

delicious disgusting salty sour
spicy sweet

5 Complete the sentences with the words in the Vocabulary box.

1 The chef has used too much salt and the biscuits are too *salty*.
2 Can I have another sandwich? They're ________ !
3 Don't eat this old smelly fish. It's ________ !
4 This chocolate has got chilli in it. I love ________ things.
5 There's a lot of sugar in the cake, so it's very ________ .
6 I don't like lemons and other ________ fruit.

Fun Spot

6 Work in groups. Invent three ice cream flavours. Tell the class about them. Vote for the most delicious and the most disgusting flavours.

Our first ice cream flavour is fish and chips.

Listening and Writing

I can understand and write a recipe.

1 **I know that!** Look at the pictures in Exercise 2. Name the food items. Which of them do you usually have in your kitchen?

2 3.18 Sidney wants to make lunch for his parents. Listen and tick the ingredients that he needs.

1 ☑

2 ☐

3 ☐

4 ☐

5 ☐

6 ☐

7 ☐

8 ☐

9 ☐

3 **Exam Spot** 3.18 Listen again and complete the recipe.

Easy Frittata Recipe

Peel, boil and slice [1]*two* potatoes.

Slice one [2]________ .

[3]________ five eggs. Add salt and pepper.

Put some oil in a [4]________ . Add the eggs, the potatoes and the tomato. Cook the frittata for two or three minutes.

Then put [5]________ grams of cheese on the frittata.

Cook the frittata for a few more [6]________ .

4 Do you think Sidney's frittata is tasty? What other ingredients can you add to it?

5 Read the recipe from a food blog. Do you think it's easy?

A great apple cake!

I've made hundreds of cakes, but this recipe is the easiest! And it's delicious!

Ingredients:

1 *170 grams of sugar* *3 large eggs*
170 grams of flour *3 large apples*

Things you need:

2 a sharp knife, a spoon or an electric mixer, a large bowl and a cake tin.

Instructions:

3 Beat the eggs and sugar with a spoon for 15 minutes. If you use an electric mixer, mix for two minutes. Then add the flour and beat well. Peel the apples and chop them. Add them to the bowl. Put everything in the cake tin and bake the cake in the oven at 160°C for 30 minutes. Simple!

Writing A recipe

1 Start with a list of ingredients.
2 Write a list of other things you need, e.g. a knife, a bowl.
3 Write the instructions. Use the imperative, e.g. *Beat the eggs and sugar.*

6 Read the Writing box. Then go to page 112 and complete the instructions.

7 **Writing Time** Write a recipe for pasta with tomato sauce. Use the pictures and instructions in Exercise 6 to help you.

Find ideas
List the ingredients and other things you need.

Draft
Write the recipe.

Check and write
Check that you include all the important information and that you use the imperative for instructions. Then write the final version of the recipe.

Vocabulary

1 Write cooking verbs and nouns.

1 P_e_ _e_ _l_ the potatoes. Then b_ _ _ them for 15 minutes in hot water.
2 B_ _ _ the cake in a small cake t_ _ for 25 minutes.
3 S_ _ _ _ the bread and make ten pieces of toast.
4 Roast the chicken and potatoes in a hot o_ _ _.
5 C_ _ _ the tomatoes into small pieces.
6 Fry the eggs in a large f_ _ _ _ _ p_ _.
7 M_ _ the butter and sugar together.
8 B_ _ _ the eggs. Then a_ _ flour and milk.

2 Label the objects with the words in the box.

bowl cup fork glass knife mug plate ~~pot~~ spoon

1 _pot_
2 ______
3 ______
4 ______
5 ______
6 ______
7 ______
8 ______
9 ______

3 Complete the sentences with the words in the box.

delicious disgusting ~~salty~~ sour spicy sweet

1 I don't like these crisps. They're too _salty_.
2 Yummy! This fruit salad is ______.
3 I can't eat lemons. They're too ______.
4 I love ______ things like honey and sugar.
5 I don't want meat with chilli. I don't like ______ food.
6 Yuk! The sandwich is ______ and I can't eat it.

Pronunciation

4 3.19 Listen and repeat: /uː/.

What's my name?
My name is Lucy.
That's my food.
It's fruit – it's juicy!

Grammar

5 Complete the text with the Present Perfect form of the verbs in brackets.

July 1st
Phew! I'm tired! We [1] _have done_ (do) a lot this evening, but now it's nearly time for bed. Our guests [2] ______ (go) home. They [3] ______ (not eat) all the food, so we don't have to cook tomorrow! Dave [4] ______ (wash) the dirty dishes and I [5] ______ (put) them away. Dad [6] ______ (not clean) the barbecue and we [7] ______ (not tidy) the living room. That can wait.

6 In your notebook, write questions and answers.

1 Judy / finish her homework? ✔
Has Judy finished her homework?
Yes, she has.
2 you / ever / roast a chicken? ✘
Have you ever roasted a chicken?
No, I haven't. I have never roasted a chicken.
3 Eddie / ever / play chess? ✔
4 the children / have dinner? ✔
5 you / ever / make pancakes? ✘
6 Ann / set the table? ✘

Communication

7 3.20 Put the dialogue in the correct order. Then listen and check.

☐ I'd like some orange juice, please.
1 Wow! I'm thirsty!
☐ What programme would you like to watch?
☐ Would you like orange juice or cola?
☐ I don't mind. You choose.
☐ I'd prefer to watch TV. It's too hot to go outside.
☐ Here you are. Now, would you like to watch TV or play football?

Check yourself!

- I can talk about cooking food. ☐
- I can use the Present Perfect. ☐
- I can talk about preferences. ☐

Reading and Writing

1 **Exam Spot** Read the text and circle the correct answer a, b or c.

Tea

Tea is a very popular drink in ¹___ countries. People drink it at home, in tea shops and at school or work. They ²___ it hot, cold or with ice and some people like it sweet or spicy!

A legend says how the Emperor Shennong in ancient China first discovered tea. One day, he was sitting under a tea tree. He ³___ some water in a pot to drink. Dry leaves from the tea tree ⁴___ into his hot water! He tried the water and it was very tasty.

Tea is easy to make. ⁵___ a tea bag in a cup, glass or mug. ⁶___ some boiling water. You ⁷___ have to wait long. After a few minutes your hot drink is ready!

Scientists believe green tea is good for your blood and that black tea helps your brain. Have you got a cold? Then you ⁸___ try lemon tea. But be careful – you ⁹___ put too much sugar in it because too much sugar is bad for you!

	a	b	c
1	a much	(b) many	c any
2	a enjoy	b enjoyed	c enjoys
3	a boiled	b boil	c boils
4	a fell	b fall	c falling
5	a Find	b Do	c Put
6	a Beat	b Chop	c Add
7	a do	b don't	c not
8	a shouldn't	b should	c don't
9	a shouldn't	b should	c no

2 **Exam Spot** Write 60–80 words, giving advice about what to do (✔) and what not to do (✘) when you have a bad cold. Use these ideas to help you.

1 see a doctor (✔)
2 keep warm (✔)
3 do sports (✘)
4 (your idea) (✔)
5 (your idea) (✘)

When you have a bad cold, you should …
You shouldn't … You have to … You don't have to …

Listening

3 **Exam Spot** 3.21 Listen and tick (✔) the correct answer a, b or c.

1 What's the matter with Mary?

a ☑ b ☐ c ☐

2 What's the matter with Mr Sullivan?

a ☐ b ☐ c ☐

3 Where are the plates?

a ☐ b ☐ c ☐

4 How many cakes has Joe's mum baked today?

a ☐ b ☐ c ☐

5 What does Joe's mum want him to do?

a ☐ b ☐ c ☐

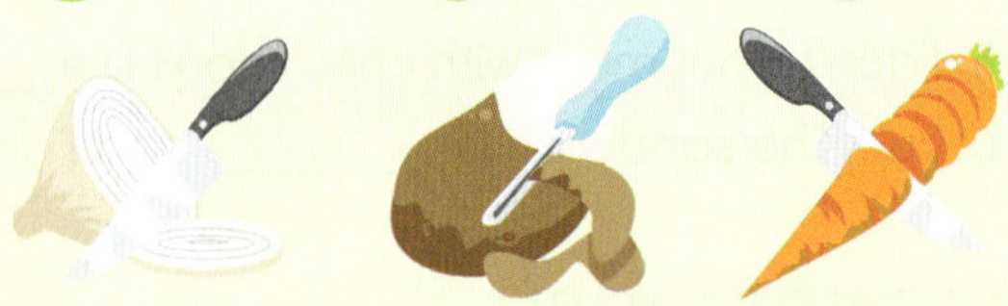

6 What time does Joe have to leave?

a ☐ b ☐ c ☐

Communication

4 Exam Spot **Betty's mum asks her some questions. Read Betty's answers and write her mum's questions.**

Mum: [1] *Would you like to stay at home or go out for lunch?*

Betty: I'd like to stay at home, please. I don't want to go out for lunch.

Mum: [2] ______________________?

Betty: I'd prefer pasta. We had chicken yesterday.

Mum: [3] ______________________?

Betty: I don't mind. I like lemonade and cola.

Mum: [4] ______________________?

Betty: A dessert? No thanks. I don't feel very well.

Mum: [5] ______________________?

Betty: I've got a headache.

Mum: [6] ______________________?

Betty: Yes, that's a good idea. I can lie down.

5 Exam Spot **Ask and answer the questions in pairs.**

1 What's your favourite food? Do you know how to make it?
2 Have you ever done anything dangerous? What?
3 What do you have to do when you get home today?
4 What exercise do you do every day?

Exam Language Bank

Health problems

Nouns
a blocked nose
a cold
a cough
a headache
a runny nose
a sore throat
a stomachache
a temperature
earache
toothache

Verbs
cough
sneeze

Injuries

broken leg
bruise
burn
cut
mosquito bite

The body

blood
bones
brain
heart
muscles

Cooking verbs

add
bake
beat
boil
chop
fry
mix
peel
roast
slice

Cooking nouns

bowl
cake tin
frying pan
oven
pot

Serving and eating food

cup
fork
glass
knife
mug
plate
spoon

Describing food

delicious
disgusting
salty
sour
spicy
sweet

Giving health advice

Asking about health
What's the matter? / What's wrong?

Responding
I don't feel very well. / I feel terrible.
I've got a *headache*/*cut*.

Giving advice
Why don't you *lie down* / *take a painkiller* / *drink some mint tea*?
Put *some cream* / *some ice* / *a plaster* on it.
I think you should see the *doctor*/*dentist*.

Accepting advice
Yes, that's a good idea. / Yes, you're right.

Preferences

Asking about preferences
Would you like to *have a picnic* or *go for a bike ride*?
Would you like *cheese* or *tuna*?

Responding
I'd like to *go for a bike ride*.
I'd like *cheese*. / I'd prefer *cheese*.
You choose. / I don't mind.

7 Where I live

Vocabulary I can talk about the place where I live.

In this unit

Vocabulary
- Places to live
- Parts of the house
- In the house
- Phrasal verbs

Grammar
- Present Continuous for future arrangements
- *must, mustn't, can*

35-36 7.2 Grammar video

37 7.2 Grammar animation

38 7.3 Grammar animation

39 7.4 Communication video

40 BBC Culture video

1 Work in pairs. How many rooms and parts of the house can you name?

Rooms: *bedroom, …* Parts of the house: *door, …*

I know that!

Home sweet home

My name is Alice and this is my school project about people's homes. You can read about my home. I also asked some friends to tell me about their homes. See how we live.

I live in Bristol in a [1] ____________. My bedroom is next to our neighbours' daughter's bedroom. I can hear the music she plays. Fortunately, we like the same music!

Beth

Hi, I'm Beth. I live in a [2] ____________ in Bristol too. It's a great city. I love the view from my room.

Paul

I'm Paul. I live in a [3] ____________ in Beverley. It's a small town in the north of England.

Kate

My name's Kate. My family and I live in a [4] ____________ in an English village. The house is about 200 years old!

Matt

I'm Matt. I live in a [5] ____________ on the Isle of Skye in Scotland. I love living on an island.

2 3.22 Listen and repeat. What types of houses can you see on page 82?

Vocabulary Places to live

Types of houses

block of flats / flat   cottage   detached house
semi-detached house   terraced house

Locations

in a city   in the country   in a town
in a village   on an island

3 3.23 Read Alice's project on page 82 and complete the texts with the types of houses. Then listen and check.

4 Label the pictures with the locations.

1 – in a village

5 3.24 Listen and repeat. Look at the houses on page 82 and answer the questions.

Vocabulary Parts of the house

attic   balcony   basement   lift   stairs
ground/first/top floor

1 Which building has a balcony?
the block of flats
2 Which buildings have an attic?
3 How many floors can you see in the block of flats?
4 Can you see a basement?
5 Which building has a lift?
6 Which buildings have stairs?

6 **Exam Spot** Read more about Beth's home. Circle the correct answer a, b or c.

My home
by Beth Barber

I live in a big [1]___ of flats in the city. My flat is on the tenth [2]___, so I always use the [3]___ to go up. I never walk up the [4]___ ! I don't have a garden, but I can sit on the [5]___ outside my bedroom when the weather is good. From there, I can see Oliver's house. He's my best friend. He lives in a [6]___ house. All the houses in his street look the same, but Oliver's has a blue door. I don't mind living in a flat, but one day, I'd like to live in a small [7]___ on a beautiful island.

	a	b	c
1	(a) block	b attic	c basement
2	a floor	b lift	c ground
3	a stairs	b basement	c lift
4	a attic	b lift	c stairs
5	a ground	b balcony	c basement
6	a terraced	b cottage	c city
7	a block	b cottage	c terraced

7 3.25 Listen to an interview with Jack and Lily. Complete the factfiles about their homes.

	Jack	Lily
Place	[1] *in the country*	[4] ______
Type of house	[2] ______	[5] ______
Garden	yes, big	[6] ______
Bedroom	in the [3] ______	upstairs

I remember that!

8 Complete the sentences so they are true for you. Compare in pairs.

I live in/on … (location)
My home is a … (type of house)
It has …, but it doesn't have … (parts of a house)

9 Now imagine you have moved to a new home. Complete the sentences in Exercise 8 again.

 I can use the Present Continuous to talk about future arrangements.

We're meeting at six o'clock

1

Emma: Are you coming to George and Harry's this evening?
Poppy: Oh, is it today?
Emma: Yes. The final of *The Greatest Voice*, our favourite talent show, is today. We're all watching it together. We're meeting at six o'clock. Remember?
Poppy: Yes, of course I'm coming. I have to go now. Mum and Dad are picking me up in two minutes. They want to show me something.
Emma: OK. See you later!
Poppy: Bye!

Later that day.

2

Emma: Hi.
Poppy: Hi. Erm … Emma, I've got some news.
Emma: Good or bad?
Poppy: It depends … We're moving house!
Emma: Oh, Poppy, no! But we live so close now!
Poppy: Yes, but the new house is bigger. And I'm getting the coolest bedroom! It's up in the attic!
Emma: Well, I'm happy for you. Wait! Please tell me you're not changing school too!
Poppy: Don't worry. I'm not changing school.
Emma: So, when are you moving?
Poppy: Next month.
Emma: And where is the new house?
Poppy: Look at this photo.
Emma: But that is … no way!

1 35 3.26 **Watch or listen and read. What's Poppy's news?**

2 Read the sentences. Circle T (true) or F (false).

1 *The Greatest Voice* is a TV show. T / F
2 Poppy says she can't go to Harry and George's today. T / F
3 Poppy is in a hurry to catch the bus. T / F
4 Emma's house is near Poppy's old house. T / F
5 Poppy loves her new bedroom. T / F
6 Poppy has to go to a different school. T / F

3 3.27 **Listen and repeat. Find the expressions in the story.**

Say it!

Remember? See you later!
It depends.

4 Guess! **Why does Emma say 'No way'?**

a Because she doesn't like the house.
b Because she knows the house.

5 36 3.28 **Now watch or listen and check.**

Grammar Present Continuous for future arrangements

+	Poppy **is moving** house next month. We**'re meeting** at six o'clock.
–	Poppy **isn't going** home after school. Poppy and Emma **aren't leaving** school together today.
?	**Are** you **coming** to George and Harry's this evening? Yes, I **am**. / No, I**'m not**.
	When **are** you **moving**?

Time expressions

today, tonight, this evening, this week
tomorrow, tomorrow morning, tomorrow evening
next week, next month
in five minutes, at six o'clock, after school

▶ 37 Get Grammar!

6 In your notebook, write sentences. Who's got the most exciting plan for the weekend?

1 Harry / play / tennis / on Saturday and Sunday.
Harry is playing tennis on Saturday and Sunday.
2 George / spend / Sunday / with his friend, David.
3 Mr and Mrs Nichols / fly / to Paris for the weekend.
4 Emma and Gran / tidy / the basement / tomorrow.
5 Poppy's parents / buy / a bed for her new room / this weekend.

7 Complete the dialogue with the Present Continuous form of the verbs in the box.

come do not do ~~go~~ have not meet tidy

Emma: Sorry, Poppy, but I can't come to drama class after school. Gran and I [1] *are going* shopping.
Poppy: Oh, I forgot to tell you. The teacher's got the flu. We [2] ________ today. What [3] ______ you ________ tomorrow morning? Do you want to meet?
Emma: I [4] ________ my first piano lesson! Then Gran and I [5] ________ the basement.
Poppy: What about Sunday? [6] ______ you ________ to the cinema with us?
Emma: Yes, I am. I [7] ________ anything else on Sunday!

8 Work in pairs. Imagine today it is Thursday 10th. Look at Mrs Nichols' diary. Take turns to ask and answer questions. Use the expressions in the box.

today at half past one
this evening
tomorrow evening
on Saturday morning
on Saturday afternoon
on Sunday
next week

Thur 10	1.30 p.m. have lunch with Beth Ellis 9.00 p.m. pick up Harry from tennis
Fri 11	8.00 p.m. go to the cinema with Peter
Sat 12	11.15 a.m. see the dentist 5.00 p.m. go to the gym
Sun 13	tidy the garden
Mon 14	go on a business trip to Madrid
Tue 15	

A: *What is Mrs Nichols doing today at half past one?*
B: *She's having lunch with Beth Ellis.*

Fun Spot

9 Tell your partner three things you are doing in the nearest future – two true and one false. Your partner guesses the false sentence.

A: *I'm singing in a talent show this weekend.*
B: *False. You aren't singing in a talent show!*
A: *No, I'm not. You're right!*

Doctor Q House rules

1 **I know that!** **Which pieces of furniture can you see in the cartoon?**

armchair bath bed chair desk fridge sofa table wardrobe

2 **3.29 Read and listen. Who is the messiest person in Doctor Q's house?**

3 **Read again. Complete the sentences.**

1 Doctor Q is looking for his *umbrella* .
2 __________ found it in the kitchen.
3 Everyone gets a __________ when they put things away.
4 The __________ in the armchair aren't Rob's.
5 Millie can use Doctor Q's __________ and drawer.
6 In the end, __________ hasn't got any stickers.

Grammar *must, mustn't, can*

must
I/You/He/She/It **must** try harder.
We/You/They **must** try harder.
mustn't
I/You/He/She/It **mustn't** make a mess.
We/You/They **mustn't** make a mess.
can
I/You/He/She/It **can** use my desk.
We/You/They **can** use my desk.

▶ 38 Get Grammar!

4 Read Doctor Q's lab rules. Circle the correct answer.

Before we leave the lab

1 We *(must)* / *mustn't* put the books back in their place.
2 We *must* / *mustn't* tidy up the lab desk.
3 We *must* / *mustn't* forget to turn off the lab computers.
4 We *must* / *mustn't* leave any rubbish on the floor.
5 We *must* / *mustn't* turn off all the lights.

5 3.30 Complete the dialogue with *mustn't* or *can*. Then listen and check.

Pi: [1] *Can* I play a computer game?
Rob: Not here, Pi. You [2] ________ touch the lab computer.
Pi: Why not? You and Millie [3] ________ use it.
Rob: It's only for work, Pi. We [4] ________ play games on it. You [5] ________ take this tablet.
Pi: OK. Oh, there's *Rock Band*! I love this game!
Rob: You [6] ________ make too much noise because we're working. Here, you [7] ________ put on these headphones.
Pi: Yay!

6 3.31 Listen and repeat. Look at the cartoon and find the items from the Vocabulary box.

Vocabulary In the house

bookcase cupboard drawer mirror sink tap

7 Complete the notes with the words in the Vocabulary box.

Doctor Q, you must put the dirty dishes in the kitchen [1] *sink*! *Millie*

Pi, you can use my dictionary, but please put it back in the [2] ________. *Doctor Q*

Doctor Q, you must check how you look in the [3] ________ before you go out. *Millie*

Pi, you must put the cereal box in the [4] ________ after breakfast! Don't leave it on the table! *Rob*

Pi, you can put your stickers in the big [5] ________ of my desk. *Doctor Q*

Doctor Q, you mustn't forget to turn off the [6] ________ after you wash your hands! *Pi*

8 Think about the rules in your house. Complete the sentences. Compare in small groups. Are the rules similar?

I must … I mustn't … I can …

I can make, accept and decline invitations.

I'm sorry, we can't come

George: Hi, David. What's up?
David: Hi, George. Mum's taking us to the adventure park on Saturday. Can you and Harry come? We can take two more people in the car.
George: That sounds fun. But we have to ask our parents first.
Harry: Ask our parents what?
George: David's asking if we can go to the adventure park on Saturday.
Harry: We're going to Aunt Alice's this Saturday … I think.
George: I'm sorry, David, we can't come. We're visiting our cousins. Are you free on Sunday? Would you like to hang out?
David: Yes, I'd love to, thanks.
George: Great. See you on Sunday then.
David: Bye.

A few seconds later …
Harry: George, I've checked it with Dad, Aunt Alice is Saturday next week. Quick, call David back.

1 39 3.32 **Watch or listen and read. Answer the questions.**

1 Where's David going on Saturday?
2 Why does George say that he and Harry can't go with David?

2 3.33 **Listen and repeat.**

Communication Invitations

Making an invitation

Mum's taking us to the adventure park on Saturday. Can you come?
Are you free on *Sunday*? Would you like to *hang out*?
Do you want to *hang out on Sunday*?

Accepting an invitation

That sounds *fun/great*. Thank you.
Yes, I'd love to, thanks.

Declining an invitation

I'm sorry, I can't (come). I'm busy *on Saturday*.
I'd love to, but *we're visiting our cousins this Saturday*.
Sorry, maybe next time.

3 3.34 **Complete the dialogues with sentences a–e. Then listen and check.**

a Are you free this afternoon?
b Do you want to hang out on Friday evening?
c Maybe next time.
d That sounds fun.
e Would you like to come?

1 A: Freddie and I are going to town this afternoon. Can you come with us?
B: Sorry, Mum and I are visiting Grandpa. [1] *c*
2 A: Hi, Jen. [2] ______
B: Yes, I'd love to, thanks.
3 A: Uncle Joe is taking us to the beach on Saturday. [3] ______
B: I'm sorry, I can't. I'm busy on Saturday.
4 A: [4] ______ Would you like to go cycling with me?
B: I'd love to, but I have a music lesson. What about tomorrow? We can go cycling in the park.
A: [5] ______ .

4 **Work in pairs. Take turns to make invitations and accept or decline them. Use the ideas below or your own ideas.**

1 parents / take us / camping / weekend – can / come?
A: *My parents are taking us camping this weekend. Can you come?*
B: *I'd love to, but I'm going to the beach on Saturday.*
2 free / this evening? – would like / watch / a DVD / with me?
3 you / want / cinema / Friday evening?
4 would like / hang out / this afternoon?
5 have / barbecue / this weekend – can / come?

What can you do to make your neighbourhood a better place?

LET'S FIND OUT!

1 ☐ Is your neighbourhood clean?

Everyone loves a clean neighbourhood, so please don't drop litter in the street. Don't expect someone else to pick it up for you. Look for a bin and put it in there. You can also take it with you and put it in the bin at home. Are you taking your dog for his usual walk this afternoon? You mustn't leave the house without a little bag. Clean up after your dog and be a good example for your neighbours.

2 ☐ Is your neighbourhood green?

Flowers and trees make your neighbourhood pretty and a healthy place to live. Do you have a garden? Why don't you plant flowers in front of your house? No garden? No problem! You can easily plant flowers in flower pots on your balcony. You mustn't forget to water them, though!

3 ☐ Is your neighbourhood friendly to wildlife?

When we wake up and hear birds singing, we feel happy and relaxed. They are also useful because they eat insects. So how can you make your neighbourhood friendly to birds? A good start is to leave some food for them, especially in winter, and put clean water in a bird bath every day. They need it for drinking and washing.

For lots of other ideas check out our website:
www.teens4abetterneighb

1 Look at pictures A–C. What are the children doing?

2 3.35 Read and listen to the text. Match pictures A–C to paragraphs 1–3.

3 **Exam Spot** Read the text again. Complete the sentences. Use one, two or three words.

1 You should take your litter home with you or put it in a *bin*.
2 When you take your dog for a walk, don't forget to take ________.
3 It is a good idea to plant flowers in front of ________.
4 Put flowers in flower pots on your balcony and ________ them.
5 It is good to have birds in a garden because they ________ and sing.
6 Birds need water for drinking and ________.

4 3.36 Listen and repeat. Find the phrases in the text. Can you guess their meaning?

Vocabulary Phrasal verbs

check out clean up find out look for wake up

5 Complete the sentences with the phrasal verbs in the Vocabulary box.

1 I can't find my dog, Buster. Please help me *look for* him.
2 Can you ________ the mess on the balcony? It looks awful!
3 I'm reading an interesting book about birds. I want to ________ more about them.
4 I ________ at half past six when my alarm clock rings.
5 ________ this blog. It's got amazing photos.

6 What's your neighbourhood like? Do you and your family do anything to make it a good place?

7.6 Listening and Writing

I can understand a text about an event
I can write an invitation to an event.

1 How well do you know your neighbours? Are you friends with them?

2 3.37 Listen to Angie talking to her cousin Mark. Which photo is from a 'neighbours afternoon' in Mark's street?

A

B

3 3.37 Listen again and answer the questions.

1 Where did Angie live in the past?
2 Where does she live now?
3 When do the people in Mark's street have a 'neighbours afternoon'?
4 What do the people switch off?
5 What day is the 'neighbours afternoon' this year?
6 What is Mark doing tomorrow?

4 What do you think of the 'neighbours afternoon'? Would you like to take part in one?

5 Read Angie's email. What is happening in the park on Saturday?

Hi Wendy,

What are you doing next Saturday? Would you like to spend the day with me?

We're having a picnic in the park across the road. Lots of people from our block of flats are coming. We're meeting at the gate at one o'clock. It's a great way to meet our neighbours, have a good time together and become friends.

We must all bring some food to the picnic: pies, sandwiches, cakes or biscuits. We can play music and dance too, but we mustn't make too much noise.

Please come!

Angie

Writing Checking for mistakes

Always remember to read through the first draft of your text to check for spelling, punctuation and grammar mistakes. Check your final draft too.

6 Read the sentences and correct the mistakes. The number of mistakes in each sentence is in brackets.

1 He live in a teraced house in London. (2)
He lives in a terraced house in London.
2 Can yu come to my house on Friday. (2)
3 Our neghbours having a party tonight. (2)
4 I baked a cake some cupcaks and some biscits. (3)
5 You mustn't arriving late! (1)
6 We're meeting at two oclock. (1)

7 Writing Time Imagine you have moved to a new house. You and your family want to have a party for friends. Write an email to a friend and invite him/her.

Find ideas

Think about the arrangements you for the party. Use these questions to help you:
Who's coming?
Why are you having the party?
What can you do to have fun at the party?
Is there something you must or mustn't do?

Draft

Invite your friend to the party and tell him/her about the arrangements you have made.

Check and write

Make sure you check spelling, grammar and punctuation.
Write the final version of your email.

Vocabulary

1 Complete the texts with the words in the box.

attic balcony cottage country block floor lift ~~terraced~~

This home is a [1]*terraced* house in Green Street. It has two bedrooms on the first [2]________ and two more bedrooms in the [3]________ .

Come and see this home in a [4]________ of flats. There is a fantastic view from the [5]________ . The building has a [6]________ .

If you like living in the [7]________ , you must come and see this beautiful [8]________ !

2 Complete the sentences with things in the house.

1 Don't waste water. Turn off the t*ap* !
2 Put the jam away in the c__________ .
3 Do you want to brush your hair? There's a m__________ in the hall.
4 The s__________ is full of dirty plates.
5 Please put these books back in the b__________ .
6 My socks are in the third d__________ .

3 Circle the correct answer.

1 We must clean *down* / (*up*) the mess.
2 Wake *up* / *on* ! It's 7.30!
3 We want to find *up* / *out* some information about these flowers.
4 What are you looking *out* / *for*?
5 Let's go and check *out* / *up* the new pet shop.

Pronunciation

4 3.38 Listen and repeat.

Can you hear an 's' in 'island'?
Can you hear a 'k' in 'know'?
Can you hear a 'p' in 'cupboard'?
No, I can't, no!

Grammar

5 Complete the email with the Present Continuous form of the verbs in brackets.

Hi Gemma,
You asked about our plans for the weekend. Well, I [1]*'m meeting* (meet) Alfie and we [2]________ (play) chess together tomorrow afternoon. We [3]________ (not have) dinner at home tomorrow evening. We [4]________ (go) to that new Italian restaurant in Long Street. Dad [5]________ (not work) this weekend. He and Mum [6]________ (visit) Granny on Sunday.
What about you? What [7]________ (you / do) tomorrow and on Sunday?
Tom

6 Complete the sentences with *must*, *mustn't* or *can*.

1 You *must* feed the animals now. They're hungry.
2 Yes, you ________ use my phone. No problem.
3 You ________ make a noise! The baby is sleeping.
4 You ________ forget to water the plants.
5 You ________ tidy the kitchen. It's very messy!
6 Are you feeling cold? You ________ close the window. I don't mind.

Communication

7 3.39 Complete the dialogues with the words in the box. Then listen and check.

~~Can~~ free want love maybe sounds

1 A: Dad's taking me to the zoo this weekend. [1]*Can* you come?
B: I'm sorry, I can't, [2]________ next time.
2 A: Do you [3]________ to hang out this afternoon?
B: I'd [4]________ to, but I'm visiting my cousins.
3 A: Are you [5]________ next Sunday? Would you like to come to my house for a barbecue?
B: That [6]________ fun. Thank you.

Check yourself!

- I can talk about the place where I live. ☐
- I can use the Present Continuous for future arrangements. ☐
- I can use *must*, *mustn't* and *can*. ☐
- I can make, accept and decline invitations. ☐

Get Culture!

Food to try in the UK

Very British food

1 ☐
It's a type of sweet. It is made with sugar, it comes in many flavours and colours and it usually has words written inside it. It is very popular in seaside holiday places, like Brighton. Look carefully at the photo – can you read the words inside the stick?

2 ☐
People first made it in Scotland, about 900 years ago! The recipe we use now is very simple: all you need is flour, butter and sugar. In the old times, shortbread was very expensive and most people only had it on special days, like the first day of the New Year. Now you can buy it almost everywhere in the world.

3 ☐
This very tasty snack comes from Wales. It's also called 'Welsh rabbit', but it has no rabbit in it at all! Welsh rarebit is very easy to make at home. You make a mixture with cheese, butter, mustard and flour, put it on top of toasted bread and then under a hot grill. There are recipes for Scottish and English rarebit too!

4 ☐
It has a strong smell and salty taste, but it also has a lot of fans around the world. People usually eat it with crackers after a good dinner. The cheese in the photo is called Blue Stilton. They make it in the East Midlands. Here's a fun fact: it takes ten litres of milk to make just one kilo of cheese!

1 Look at the photos. What types of food can you see?

2 Read texts 1–4 quickly. Match the names A–F to the texts. There are two extra names.

3 3.40 Listen and read about the four British products. Check your answers to Exercise 2.

4 Read the texts again. Circle T (true) or F (false).

1 Rock has got sugar in it. (T) / F
2 The only place where you can find rock is Brighton. T / F
3 Scottish shortbread has got eggs in it. T / F
4 You can eat shortbread only in Scotland. T / F
5 Welsh rarebit is very difficult to make. T / F
6 There's no meat in Welsh rarebit. T / F
7 Stilton cheese is salty. T / F
8 People usually eat Stilton before their dinner. T / F

5 3.41 Listen to two people from different parts of the UK. Circle the correct answers.

1 Gavin is from the (*southeast*) / *southwest* of England.
2 You *need* / *don't need* milk to make Yorkshire pudding.
3 Gavin likes eating Yorkshire pudding with *eggs* / *roast beef*.
4 Morwenna is talking about a *Scottish* / *Cornish* dish.
5 Stargazy pie has *beef* / *fish* in it.
6 Morwenna says a lot of people *like* / *don't like* stargazy pie.

6 Which of the two dishes in Exercise 5 would you like to try? Why?

British takeaway food

A 40 **Watch the video and answer the presenter's question. Which of these takeaway foods is not in the video? Circle the correct answer a, b, c or d.**

a Indian food **b** pizza **c** Chinese food **d** fish and chips

B 40 **Watch the video again. Complete the sentences with one or two words.**

1 British people spend ________ billion pounds on takeaways every year.
2 People buy takeaway food because they haven't got ________ to ________ .
3 You make fish and chips batter with ________ , salt and water.
4 A wok is a type of large ________ ________ .
5 The first Indian restaurant opened in London in ________ .

C **Which type of takeaway food is your favourite? If you haven't tried any, which one would you like to eat? Discuss your answers as a class.**

PROJECT

- **Work in groups. Think of different areas of your country and the popular dishes. Use the words below to help you.**

sweets/desserts meals, e.g. breakfast or dinner traditional dishes drinks

- **Write about the food that people make or eat there. Use these questions to help you:**
  What kind of food is the place famous for?
  What do people use to make the food?
  What does it taste like?
- **Find some photos and put them together with the text to make a page of a food guide.**
- **Present your page to the class. Put all the pages in one document. Which is your favourite page? Why?**

8 A happy life

Vocabulary I can talk about life ambitions.

In this unit

Vocabulary
- Life ambitions
- Being with people
- Good manners

Grammar
- *will* for predictions
- Questions and question words

8.2 Grammar video

8.2 Grammar animation

8.3 Grammar animation

8.4 Communication video

I know that!

1 How important are these things for you? Order them from 1 to 6, starting with the most important.

- ☐ have a lot of friends
- ☐ do well at school
- ☐ read a lot of books
- ☐ have a hobby
- ☐ be good at sports
- ☐ travel abroad

I wanted to be a superhero!

Hi, my name is Ricky. Yesterday, I found some photos. Look! Some of them are old. Wow! I've changed a lot!

In this photo, I'm five. That's my sister. She wanted to *be* / *have* a doctor. I wanted to be a superhero!

At the age of seven, I was crazy about cars and I wanted to *have* / *learn* to drive more than anything in the world.

When I was fifteen, I decided to *learn* / *live* a new foreign language, so I started taking Spanish lessons. Here I am on holiday in Spain.

When I was twenty-one, my greatest ambition was to *have* / *live* on my own. My first flat was very small and cold!

Now I'm thirty-five. I'm lucky – I *learn* / *have* an interesting job. I'm an artist. My daughter took this photo. She's six and she wants to be a photographer.

2 Read about Ricky on page 94 and look at the pictures. How old is Ricky in each picture? Find the answers in his comments.

3 3.42 Listen and repeat.

Vocabulary Life ambitions

be	a doctor / famous / rich
have	a family / an interesting job / my own business
learn	a foreign language / to drive
live	abroad / on my own

4 3.43 Read Ricky's comments on page 94 and circle the correct answer. Then listen and check.

5 3.44 Look at the pictures of Ricky's sister, Kate. Complete the text. Use the Vocabulary box to help you. Then listen and check.

That's my sister, Kate. She's an actor and she's [1]*famous*. She doesn't live in the UK. She lives [2]________, so I don't see her often. Kate has a great [3]________. Her husband, Wally, is American. He has his own [4]________. They're very [5]________. They even have their own plane!

6 3.45 Listen and match people 1–3 to their ambitions when they were younger a–e. Then make sentences.

1 Jake
2 Sally
3 Elsa

a be famous
b learn foreign languages
c have a family
d live on his/her own
e live abroad

Jake wanted to have a family and …

7 Complete the phrases with the correct verb from the Vocabulary box.

1 *be*: a pilot, a teacher, happy
2 ________: in the UK, in a big city, near my family
3 ________: a house with a garden, good health, fun
4 ________: Chinese, to fly, to play the drums

8 Exam Spot Complete Olivia's blog post with one word in each gap.

My ambitions
by Olivia Reeves

My greatest dream is to travel, so I want to [1]*learn* two or three foreign languages.

I don't want to be [2]________ – money isn't important to me – but I want to [3]________ happy. I'd also like to [4]________ in a big city, perhaps in New York. I'd like to meet new people and [5]________ fun. Another ambition of mine is to learn [6]________ fly. I'd love to [7]________ a pilot!

I remember that!

9 Complete the sentences. Then talk about your ambitions in pairs. Do you have similar or different ambitions?

I want to be … *I want to have …*
I want to learn … *I want to live …*

8.2 Grammar I can use *will* for predictions.

I'll present a TV show

Poppy is making a video for a class project.

Poppy: So Emma, what do you want to do in the future?
Emma: Well, I love travelling and I'd like to work on TV, so maybe I'll present a TV travel show! I'll travel all around the world!

Poppy: Will you go to the Amazon rain forest too? Can I come? It's one of my dreams!
Emma: Yes, I will. It'll be fantastic to go there together.
George: Emma won't go to the rain forest. She hates spiders and the rain forest is full of them!
Emma: Oh …

George: My turn now. One day, I'll have my own flat. You'll ask, 'Why is this so important?' Because I won't share a room with my brother anymore – he snores like a hippo!
Harry: You're so funny!

Poppy: What will you do, Harry? Will you play tennis professionally?
Harry: It's hard to decide. I love sports, but I'd also like to be a doctor like Dad.
Poppy: Hmm … Here's a thought.

1 ▶41 🔊 3.46 **Watch or listen and read. Who wants to live on his/her own in the future?**

2 Read the story. Circle T (true) or F (false).

1 Emma would like to do two things. T / F
2 Poppy wouldn't like to visit the Amazon rain forest. T / F
3 There aren't any spiders in the rain forest. T / F
4 George doesn't like sleeping in the same room as Harry. T / F
5 Harry doesn't want to be a doctor. T / F

3 🔊 3.47 **Listen and repeat. Find the expressions in the story.**

Say it!

My turn now.
It's hard to decide. Here's a thought.

4 ▶ **Guess! What is Poppy's suggestion? Compare your ideas in pairs.**

5 ▶42 🔊 3.48 **Now watch or listen and check.**

Grammar *will* for predictions

▶ 43 Get Grammar!

+	–
I/You/He/She/It'**ll travel**.	I/You/He/She/It **won't travel**.
We/You/They'**ll travel**.	We/You/They **won't travel**.
?	**Short answers**
Will I/you/he/she/it **travel**?	Yes, I/you/he/she/it **will**. / No, I/you/he/she/it **won't**.
Will we/you/they **travel**?	Yes, we/you/they **will**. / No, we/you/they **won't**.

What **will** you **do**? Where **will** they **go**?

'll = will won't = will not

Time expressions

one day, in the future, when I'm older, in ten years

6 **Complete Gran's predictions about her family. Use *will* and the phrases in the box.**

~~be a dance teacher~~ buy a cottage be a vet learn to fly a plane have a very big family

Emma loves dancing. She [1]*'ll be a dance teacher* one day.

Poppy loves animals. She [2]________________.

Harry loves children. He [3]________________.

George is mad about planes. He [4]________________ when he is older.

Angela and Peter love the country. They [5]________________ one day.

7 **In your notebook, write sentences to correct Gran's predictions.**

1 **Emma:** I'd like to be a TV presenter!
Emma won't be a dance teacher.
She'll be a TV presenter.
2 **Poppy:** I love drawing and want to be an artist.
3 **Harry:** I'd like to have two children.
4 **George:** I'd like to learn to ride my dad's motorbike!
5 **Mr and Mrs Nichols:** Our dream is to buy a house on a Greek island.

8 **In your notebook, write questions about the next school year.**

1 our school football team / win / a lot of games?
Will our school football team win a lot of games?
2 we / have / a new English teacher?
3 we / learn / another foreign language?
4 the tests / be / more difficult?
5 we / go / on a school trip abroad?
6 the classes / be / more fun?

9 **In pairs, ask and answer the questions in Exercise 8. Give your own answers.**

A: *Will our school football team win a lot of games?*
B: *Yes, they will. They're very good.*

Fun Spot

10 **Work in pairs. Student A: Make a prediction about Student B's future life. Student B: Say if you agree. Then swap roles.**

A: *You'll be a doctor.*
B: *I won't be a doctor because I don't like hospitals.*
B: *You'll live abroad.*
A: *Maybe I will. I'd like to see the world.*

Doctor Q Mrs Q's visit

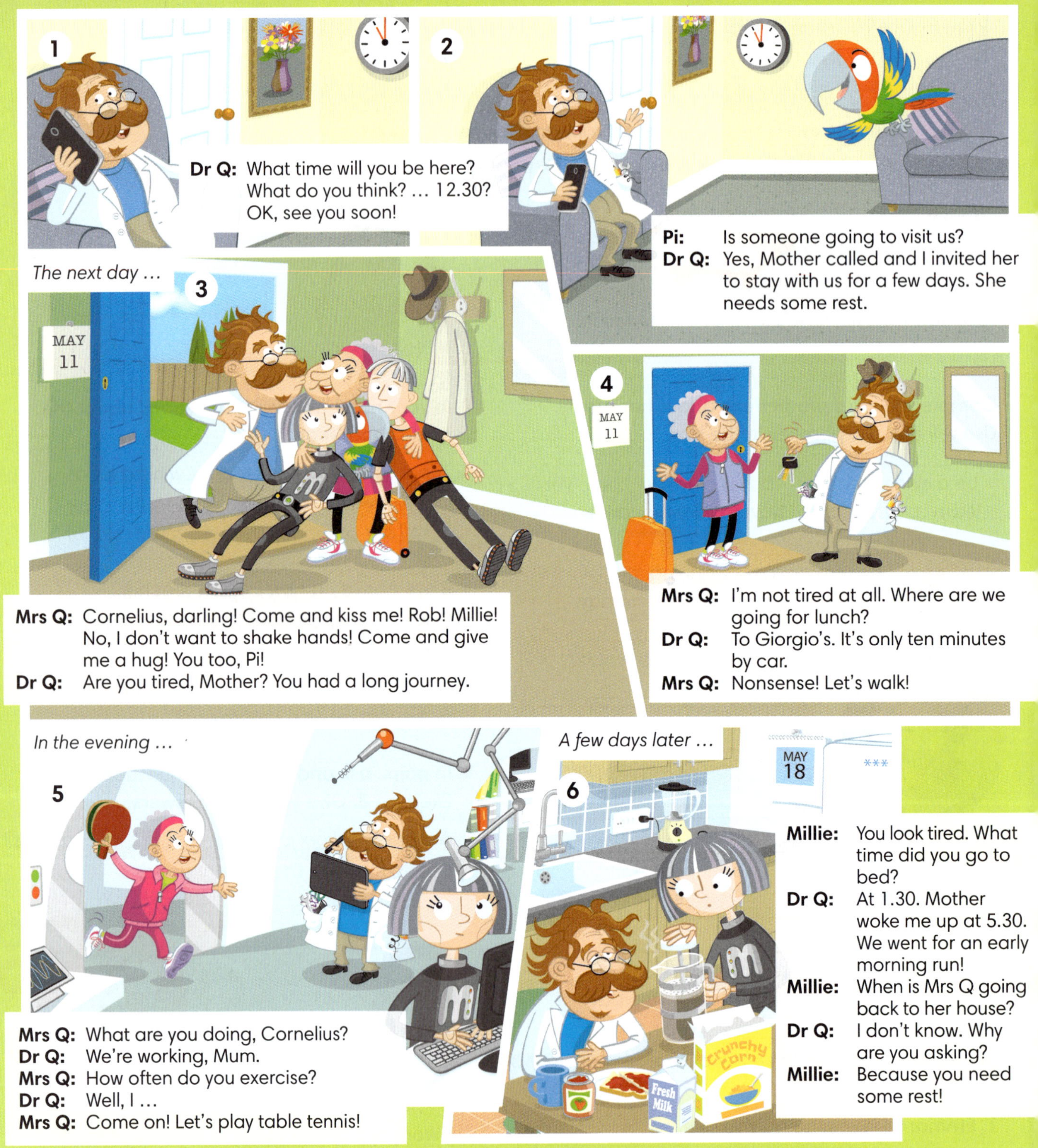

1 **Look at the cartoon. When did Mrs Q arrive? What date is it in picture 6?**

2 **3.49 Listen and read. Who's more active: Doctor Q or Mrs Q?**

3 **Read again. Complete the sentences.**

1 Doctor Q's *mother* is coming to visit him tomorrow.
2 Mrs Q is not __________ after her journey.
3 Doctor Q and Mrs Q are going out to have __________ .
4 Mrs Q doesn't want to go to the restaurant by __________ .
5 Doctor Q went for a run at __________ in the morning.

Grammar Questions and question words

Present Simple	How often **do** you **exercise**?
Present Continuous	Why **are** you **asking**?
Past Simple	Who **did** Doctor Q **invite**?
Past Continuous	What **was** Doctor Q **doing** at 5 a.m.?
will	When **will** Doctor Q **rest**?
be going to	How long **is** Mrs Q **going to** stay?

▶ 44 Get Grammar!

4 In your notebook, write questions about the cartoon. Then answer them.

Picture 1

1 Doctor Q | doing | What | at eleven o'clock | was | ?

What was Doctor Q doing at eleven o'clock?

He was talking to his mother.

2 Mrs Q | at Doctor Q's house | What | time | arrive | will | ?

Picture 2

3 is | Mrs Q | Why | stay | going to | with Doctor Q | ?

Picture 4

4 are | having | Doctor Q and Mrs Q | Where | lunch | ?

Picture 5

5 Mrs Q | does | What | to do | want | ?

Picture 6

6 Doctor Q | How many | hours | did | sleep | ?

5 3.50 Listen and repeat. Complete the sentences about the cartoon with the correct names.

Vocabulary Being with people

call give someone a hug invite kiss shake hands visit

1 *Mrs Q* called Doctor Q.

2 ________ invited Mrs Q.

3 ________ visited Doctor Q and his friends.

4 ________ kissed Mrs Q.

5 ________ and ________ wanted to shake hands with Mrs Q.

6 ________ gave Millie, Rob and Pi a hug.

LOOK!

Who **did** Doctor Q **invite**?	Doctor Q invited **Mrs Q**.
Who **invited** Mrs Q?	**Doctor Q** invited Mrs Q.

6 Write questions about the sentences in Exercise 5. Begin each question with *Who*. Can you answer the questions with your book closed?

Who called Doctor Q? – Mrs Q.

Who invited …

7 3.51 Write questions about the words in bold. Listen and circle the correct answer.

1 **Mrs Q / Doctor Q** is playing the drums.
Who is playing the drums?

2 Millie was **making breakfast / dancing** at 8 a.m.

3 Doctor Q is going to visit Doctor Spark **next week / tomorrow**.

4 Mrs Q calls her son **every week / every day**.

5 Mrs Q and Pi will travel **to Africa / to the Arctic** one day.

Fun Spot

8 Work in pairs. Ask your partner three questions about his/her life with different question words in different tenses. Answer your partner's questions. Try to think of the funniest answers you can.

A: *Who woke you up today?*
B: *The Queen woke me up today.*
A: *Where will you live in fifteen years?*
B: *I will live …*

8.4 Communication

I can express agreement and disagreement.

I don't think so

Mum: George, can you turn that down, please?
George: Why? This music is awesome!
Mum: I disagree. It's giving me a headache.
George: Dad likes it!
Dad: That's true. I think the electric guitar is the most exciting musical instrument.
George: That's what I think too! Why don't we buy one?
Dad: I don't think so, George. Electric guitars cost a lot of money.
Mum: How about a second-hand one? It won't be too expensive.
George: Yes, you're right. But I thought you didn't like electric guitars.
Mum: You're wrong. I just didn't like the music they were playing on the radio.

1 45 3.52 **Watch or listen and read. Answer the questions.**

1 Does Mr Nichols like the music on the radio?
2 What does George want to buy?

2 3.53 **Listen and repeat.**

Communication
Agreeing and disagreeing

Agreeing

I agree (with you).
You're right.
That's true. / That's right.
That's what I think too.

Disagreeing

I disagree (with you).
I don't agree (with you).
You're wrong.
That's not true. / That isn't right.
I don't think so.

3 3.54 **Complete the dialogues with the words in the box. Then listen and check.**

don't right so ~~terrible~~ true wrong

1 **A:** This film is [1]*terrible*!
B: You're [2]________. Let's watch something else.
2 **A:** Everybody likes going to the beach.
B: That's not [3]________. I don't like it. It's too hot.
3 **A:** Ankara is the biggest city in Turkey.
B: You're [4]________. Istanbul is much bigger.
4 **A:** English is a very easy language.
B: I [5]________ think [6]________. I think it's difficult.

4 **Exam Spot** 3.55 **It's Mum's birthday. What is each person going to buy her? Listen and match people 1–4 to presents A–F. There are two extra presents.**

1 [*F*] Ivy 2 [ ] Dad 3 [ ] Grandad 4 [ ] Steve

A 
B 
C 
D 
E 
F 

5 Go to page 112. Compare your opinions in pairs.

Debbie's teen problem page

Late – again!

Dear Debbie,

Can you help me? It's my friend, Joe. I always arrive on time, but he's always late. Last week I was waiting for him outside the cinema. This time he was half an hour late! 'Where were you?' I asked. 'I was chatting to Freddie,' he said. He didn't even say sorry! I'm sure that in future he'll be late again. Why do people think it's OK to keep others waiting?

Derek

Being late is a common problem and it's not polite. It's important to be on time. It shows you care about other people's feelings. Speak to your friend and explain this to him. And next time you arrange to meet, say 'Please don't be late.' Then wait and see what happens.

Little brother, big problem

Dear Debbie,

My little brother is five and he's terrible. When I'm chatting to my friends, he interrupts all the time. 'When are we having dinner?', 'Where's my teddy?' He takes my things and he never asks for permission. Oh, and he always wants to be first for everything. He never waits his turn. Mum says 'He's still young. He'll learn.' But it's really annoying.

Julie

Little brothers and sisters can be annoying, but your mum is right. He is young. Be patient with your brother and keep repeating (nicely!): 'Please don't interrupt', 'Please don't take my things without asking.' He will learn.

1 **Read the problem page quickly. Circle the correct answer.**

1 Why is Derek complaining?
   a His friend talks too much.
   b His friend always keeps him waiting.
2 What does Debbie say about Julie's brother?
   a He will change when he's older.
   b He asks too many questions.

2 **3.56 Read and listen to the problem page. Answer the questions.**

1 How long did Derek wait for Joe?
2 Why was Joe late again?
3 What advice does Debbie give Derek?
4 What does Julie's brother do when she's chatting to her friends?
5 How often does he ask for permission when he takes Julie's things?
6 Who can be annoying in Debbie's opinion?

3 **3.57 Listen and repeat. Then complete the sentences with one word in each gap.**

Vocabulary Good manners

arrive on time   ask for permission   be polite
don't be late   don't interrupt   wait your turn

To all students!

1 *Be* polite to your classmates, teachers and all other staff.
2 Please arrive on ______________ .
3 ______________ be late for class meetings.
4 Wait your ______________ politely in the school canteen. Don't push!
5 Listen to your classmates and don't ______________ them when they are speaking.
6 Ask for ______________ before you borrow books from the class library.

4 **3.58 Listen to four conversations. In which conversation:**

a [ ] does someone wait their turn?
b [ ] does someone ask for permission?
c [*1*] does someone arrive on time?
d [ ] does someone interrupt?

5 **Are good manners important to you?**

8.6 Listening and Writing

I can understand and write short texts about predictions for the future.

1 In pairs, look at the pictures showing different aspects of life in the future. How will they be different from the life we know now? Tell your partner.

a ☐

home

b ☐

education

c ☐

transport

d ☐

work

e ☐

free time

f ☐

food

2 3.59 Listen to Robbie, Jen and their mum talking about the future. What do they talk about? Tick (✓) the pictures in Exercise 1.

3 3.59 Listen again. Complete the sentences.

1 *Robbie* enjoyed the film more than Jen.
2 Jen thinks the cities in the film were awful because there weren't any __________ .
3 Mum thinks people will live in different types of __________ in the future.
4 Mum thinks students will __________ online more in the future.
5 Robbie hopes there won't be __________ at schools in the future.
6 Robbie thinks people will __________ from home in the future.
7 Mum thinks people will still __________ with their friends and have hobbies.

4 Do you agree with the predictions in Exercise 3?

5 Read Gabriella's essay. Which forms of transport does it mention?

Transport in the future

by Gabriella Marques

I'm sure transport twenty-five years from now will be different. Some people think we won't use cars and we will all travel in small planes, but I don't think this will happen. I think everybody will use public transport. Maybe there will be an underground in every town and city. The streets will be for electric trams or buses and the air will be cleaner. I hope more people will ride bicycles because exercise is good for your health. When we want to visit another city or country, we will take a very fast train.

6 Read the Writing box. Find the phrases in the essay and underline them. What structure do we use after them?

Writing Making predictions

We can use these phrases to make predictions:
I think … I don't think … I'm sure …
I hope … Maybe …

7 Writing Time How do you think young people will spend their free time twenty-five years from now? Write an essay.

Find ideas

Think about technology, sports and spending time with friends and family. Make notes.
What types of technology will people use for fun?
Will people do sports in the future?
Will people spend time with friends and family?
What will they do together?

Draft

Write your essay. Use the expressions from the Writing box.

Check and write

Make sure you use words and phrases like *I think*, *I don't think*, *I'm sure*, *I hope* and *Maybe*.
Write the final draft of your essay.

Vocabulary

1 **Complete the sentences with the words in the box. There are two extra words.**

abroad ~~be~~ do famous have family learn own

I'd love to [1] *be* an actor and be [2] ________ , but I'm not talented enough.

I'm going to [3] ________ to drive when I'm older. I want to [4] ________ my own business one day.

I want to live [5] ________ , but I don't want to live there on my [6] ________ .

2 **Circle the correct answer. Ask and answer the questions in pairs.**

How are you with people?

1 When you (*visit*) / *stay* someone, do you take a gift?
2 You can't accept an invitation. Do you *speak* / *call* the person and explain why you can't come?
3 When you meet someone, do you smile and *shake* / *give* hands?
4 Did you *visit* / *invite* more than three people to your last birthday party?
5 A member of your family is upset. Do you *make* / *give* them a hug and tell them you love them?
6 When you go to bed, do you *kiss* / *make* your mum good night?

3 **Complete the words.**

1 The film starts at seven, so don't be l*ate*.
2 Please stand in the queue and wait your t_ _ _.
3 I hope Dan will arrive at the cinema on t_ _ _. He's got our tickets.
4 Parents are talking. Don't i_ _ _ _ _ _ _ _ them.
5 I'd like to use Dad's computer, but I have to ask him for p_ _ _ _ _ _ _ _ _.
6 Be p_ _ _ _ _ and say 'please' and 'thank you'.

Pronunciation

4 **3.60** **Listen and repeat: /z/ or /s/.**

Zoe and Zinia went to the zoo.
They saw some snakes and spiders too.

Grammar

5 **Complete the sentences with the correct form of *will* and the verbs in brackets.**

1 I don't think I *will pass* (pass) all my exams. My parents ________ (not be) happy.
2 When she's older, she ________ (buy) a cottage and she ________ (move) to the country.
3 What job ________ (you / do) when you finish school? ________ (you / be) famous?

6 **In your notebook, write the questions. Use the correct question word.**

1 A: you / do / this summer?
B: We're going to stay with my grandparents.
What are you going to do this summer?
2 A: visit / you / yesterday?
B: Aunt Suzan visited us yesterday.
3 A: she / move / to a new neighbourhood?
B: She's moving there next week.
4 A: they / do / yesterday at four o'clock?
B: They were watching a football match.
5 A: your best friend / live?
B: She lives next door.

Communication

7 **3.61** **Complete the dialogues with the words in the box. Then listen and check.**

disagree ~~I agree~~ I don't That's true wrong

1 A: The book was interesting.
B: *I agree* with you. I liked it too.
2 A: The city is better than the country.
B: ________ think so. I prefer the country.
3 A: Paris is bigger than Tokyo.
B: You're ________ . Tokyo is much bigger!
4 A: My sister is a better singer than me.
B: ________ , but you're better at sport.
5 A: Most people want to be famous.
B: I ________ . I think they want to be happy.

Check yourself!

- I can talk about life ambitions. ☐
- I can use *will* for predictions. ☐
- I can ask and answer questions. ☐
- I can express agreement and disagreement. ☐

Reading and Writing

Julie and her family lived in a cottage in a [1] *village* . One Saturday morning, they were having breakfast when they heard people speaking in a garden nearby. 'New neighbours!' said Julie, 'We [2] ________ invite them for lunch!' Her Mum said, 'I [3] ________ . That's a nice idea.' After that, she went next door to talk to the neighbours.

The next day, Mr and Mrs James and their son, Roy, had lunch at Julie's house. They arrived [4] ________ time and everyone shook hands. Julie said to Roy, 'Have we met before?' 'No, we haven't', said Roy. She didn't believe him because she remembered his face. After lunch Julie said to Roy, 'Would you like to hang out later?' 'That [5] ________ fun,' he said.

That evening, Julie went to her new friend's house. Roy was very nice and they talked a lot. Then Julie went home and turned on the TV. 'Mum! Dad! I don't believe it!' she said loudly. 'Roy is in a film! He's really good. I'm sure he'll [6] ________ a star one day!'

1 **Exam Spot** **Read the story. Complete the text with the words in the box. There are four extra words.**

agree	at	be	island	mustn't	on
should	sounds	~~village~~	won't		

2 **Exam Spot** **Tick (✔) the best title for the story.**

1 ☐ A new house
2 ☐ A new friend
3 ☐ An interesting lunch

3 **Exam Spot** **Write 60–80 words about how your life will change when you leave school. Use these questions to help you.**

1 Will you go to university or will you get a job?
2 Will you live on your own or share a flat with your school friends?
3 How often will you see your family?
4 What will you do in your free time?
5 Will you have an interesting job? What will it be?

I think … I don't think … I'm sure …
I hope … Maybe …

Listening

4 **Exam Spot** 3.62 **Tina and Martin are making plans for Sunday. Listen and write the answers to questions 1–8 in your notebook.**

1 Where is Tina going tomorrow?
To her uncle's new flat.
2 Which floor is the new flat on?
3 Who is Martin going to the swimming pool with?
4 What time will Tina get home tomorrow?
5 Has Martin ever been to Jack's Palace?
6 What food does Tina recommend at Jack's Palace?
7 Why did Tina's family stay at home yesterday?
8 What time are they meeting tomorrow?

Communication

5 **Exam Spot** Look at the pictures. Match a–h to 1–6. There are two extra sentences.

a I agree, but I don't like tests. Can I borrow this book?

b I've got tickets for the football match tomorrow. Would you like to come?

c Can you stay for dinner this evening? We're having roast chicken!

d We've got lots of History books! I think History is very interesting.

e I played football yesterday.

f Yes, I'd love to, thanks. I'm hungry!

g I'd love to but I must stay at home and study. I've got a History test on Monday.

h You're wrong. I don't like reading.

6 **Exam Spot** Ask and answer the questions in pairs.

1 What's your best friend's home like?

2 What must you do every morning before you go to school?

3 What are you doing next weekend?

4 Are you polite? Why do you think so?

Exam Language Bank

Places to live

Types of houses	Locations
block of flats / flat	in a city
cottage	in the country
detached house	in a town
semi-detached house	in a village
terraced house	on an island

Parts of the house

attic, balcony, basement, ground/first/top floor, lift, stairs

In the house

bookcase, cupboard, drawer, mirror, sink, tap

Phrasal verbs

check out
clean up
find out
look for
wake up

Life ambitions

be a doctor / famous / rich
have a family / an interesting job / my own business
learn a foreign language / to drive
live abroad / on my own

Being with people

call
give someone a hug
invite
kiss
shake hands
visit

Good manners

arrive on time
ask for permission
be polite
don't be late
don't interrupt
wait your turn

Invitations

Making an invitation

Mum's taking us to the adventure park on Saturday. Can you come?

Are you free on *Sunday*? Would you like to *hang out*?

Do you want to *hang out on Sunday*?

Accepting an invitation

That sounds *fun/great*. Thank you.

Yes, I'd love to, thanks.

Declining an invitation

I'm sorry, I can't (come). I'm busy *on Saturday*.

I'd love to, but *we're visiting our cousins this Saturday*.

Sorry, maybe next time.

Agreeing and disagreeing

Agreeing	Disagreeing
I agree (with you).	I disagree / don't agree (with you).
You're right.	You're wrong.
That's true. / That's right.	That's not true. / That isn't right.
That's what I think too.	I don't think so.

Student A activities

Unit 1 Lesson 1.2, Page 13, Exercise 10

Find differences between your picture and Student B's picture.

1 What's happening in your picture? Tell Student B using the verbs in the box.

~~iron~~ take out sleep text

A: *In my picture, the man is ironing.*
B: *Yes, in my picture, he's ironing too.*

2 Listen to Student B. Is the same thing or a different thing happening in your picture?

B: *In my picture, the woman is …*
A: *In my picture, she's …*

Unit 5 Lesson 5.3, Page 63, Exercise 7

1 Answer Student B's question. Use the information in the leaflet.

A: *You shouldn't camp near water.*

Going camping? Here's how to prevent mosquito bites:

- camp near water ✗
- wear light colours ✓
- wear shorts and T-shirts ✗
- use a mosquito net ✓

2 Ask Student B this question. Listen and complete the notes.

A: *What should I do to prevent burns?*

Going camping? Here's how to prevent burns:

- go near the [1] __________ ✗
- build the fire far away from the [2] __________ ✓
- touch [3] __________ pots and pans ✗
- have some [4] __________ near the fire ✓

Student A&B activities

Unit 0 Lesson 0.5, Page 9, Exercise 1

… an apple pie!

Unit 4 Lesson 4.2, Page 49, Exercise 10

Game! What were you doing yesterday at twelve o'clock? Throw a dice twice. Write sentences. Read them to the class.

1 school	1 stand in a queue
2 garden	2 **sleep**
3 **kitchen**	3 brush my teeth
4 museum	4 feed the animals
5 shop	5 looking for a friend
6 park	6 ride my bike

I was in the kitchen. I was sleeping.

Unit 6 Lesson 6.4, Page 76, Exercise 6

In pairs, complete the lists with your ideas. Then act out dialogues. Look at Exercise 5 for examples.

1 To have for dessert:
__________ or __________

2 To do now:
__________ or __________

3 To have when it's cold:
__________ or __________

4 To do this summer:
__________ or __________

5 To have for dinner tonight:
__________ or __________

Unit 0
Get started!

0.1

Vocabulary

Places in town

bank /bæŋk/
café /ˈkæfeɪ/
cinema /ˈsɪnəmə/
hospital /ˈhɒspɪtl/
hotel /həʊˈtel/
museum /mjuːˈziəm/
park /pɑːk/
restaurant /ˈrestərɒnt/
stadium /ˈsteɪdiəm/
theatre /ˈθɪətə/

Means of transport

bike /baɪk/
boat /bəʊt/
bus /bʌs/
car /kɑː/
motorbike /ˈməʊtəbaɪk/
plane /pleɪn/
taxi /ˈtæksi/
train /treɪn/
tram /træm/
underground /ˈʌndəgraʊnd/

Other

art class /ˈɑːt klɑːs/
at least /ət ˈliːst/
genius /ˈdʒiːniəs/
twice a week /ˌtwaɪs ə ˈwiːk/
unfortunately /ʌnˈfɔːtʃənətli/

0.2

Vocabulary

Jobs

artist /ˈɑːtɪst/
builder /ˈbɪldə/
bus driver /ˈbʌs ˌdraɪvə/
chef /ʃef/
doctor /ˈdɒktə/
farmer /ˈfɑːmə/
footballer /ˈfʊtbɔːlə/
nurse /nɜːs/
office worker /ˈɒfɪs ˌwɜːkə/
pilot /ˈpaɪlət/
police officer /pəˈliːs ˌɒfɪsə/
shop assistant /ˈʃɒp əˌsɪstənt/
singer /ˈsɪŋə/
teacher /ˈtiːtʃə/
vet /vet/

Other

brilliant /ˈbrɪljənt/
Here's an idea. /ˌhɪəz ən aɪˈdɪə/
indoors /ˌɪnˈdɔːz/
outdoors /ˌaʊtˈdɔːz/

0.3

Vocabulary

School subjects

Art /ɑːt/
Computer studies /kəmˈpjuːtə ˌstʌdiz/
English /ˈɪŋglɪʃ/
Geography /dʒiˈɒgrəfi/
History /ˈhɪstəri/
Maths /mæθs/
Music /ˈmjuːzɪk/
P.E. /ˌpiː ˈiː/
Science /ˈsaɪəns/

Vocabulary

Places in a school

canteen /kænˈtiːn/
classroom /ˈklɑːsrʊm/
computer room /kəmˈpjuːtə ruːm/
gym /dʒɪm/
hall /hɔːl/
library /ˈlaɪbrəri/
playground /ˈpleɪgraʊnd/
staff room /ˈstɑːf ruːm/

Other

get mad /ˌget ˈmæd/
laptop case /ˈlæptɒp keɪs/

0.4

Vocabulary

Adjectives

angry /ˈæŋgri/
bored /bɔːd/
friendly /ˈfrendli/
funny /ˈfʌni/
happy /ˈhæpi/
helpful /ˈhelpfəl/
intelligent /ɪnˈtelədʒənt/
kind /kaɪnd/
sad /sæd/
tired /taɪəd/

Adjectives with prepositions

bad at /ˈbæd ət/
good at /ˈgʊd ət/
excited about /ɪkˈsaɪtɪd əˌbaʊt/
interested in /ˈɪntrɪstɪd ɪn/
scared of /ˈskeəd əv/
worried about /ˈwʌrid əˌbaʊt/

0.5

Vocabulary

Food and drink

apple /ˈæpəl/
biscuit /ˈbɪskɪt/
bread /bred/
butter /ˈbʌtə/
carrot /ˈkærət/
cereal /ˈsɪəriəl/
chocolate /ˈtʃɒklət/
cucumber /ˈkjuːkʌmbə/
egg /eg/
flour /ˈflaʊə/
juice /dʒuːs/
orange /ˈɒrəndʒ/
rice /raɪs/
strawberry /ˈstrɔːbəri/
sugar /ˈʃʊgə/
tuna /ˈtjuːnə/
water /ˈwɔːtə/
yoghurt /ˈjɒgət/

Vocabulary

Containers

a bar of chocolate /ə ˌbɑːr əv ˈtʃɒklət/
a bottle of water /ə ˌbɒtl əv ˈwɔːtə/
a can of tuna /ə ˌkən əv ˈtjuːnə/
a carton of milk /ə ˌkɑːtn əv ˈmɪlk/
a jar of jam /ə ˌdʒɑːr əv ˈdʒæm/
a packet of flour /ə ˌpækɪt əv ˈflaʊə/

Unit 1
Life at home

1.1

Vocabulary

Household chores

clear the table /ˌklɪə ðə ˈteɪbəl/
empty the dishwasher /ˌempti ðə ˈdɪʃˌwɒʃə/
feed the dog /ˌfiːd ðə ˈdɒg/
hang out the washing /ˌhæŋ aʊt ðə ˈwɒʃɪŋ/
iron your T-shirt /ˌaɪən jə ˈtiːʃɜːt/
load the dishwasher /ˌləʊd ðə ˈdɪʃˌwɒʃə/
load the washing machine /ˌləʊd ðə ˈwɒʃɪŋ məʃiːn/
make your bed /ˌmeɪk jə ˈbed/
put away your clothes /ˌpʊt əˌweɪ jə ˈkləʊðz/
set the table /ˌset ðə ˈteɪbəl/
take out the rubbish /ˌteɪk aʊt ðə ˈrʌbɪʃ/
vacuum your room /ˌvækjuəm jə ˈruːm/
water the plants /ˌwɔːtə ðə ˈplɑːnts/

1.2

Say it!

Nice try! /ˌnaɪs ˈtraɪ/
Not really. /ˌnɒt ˈrɪəli/
Yeah, right! /ˌjeə ˈraɪt/

Other

call /kɔːl/
on my own /ˌɒn maɪ ˈəʊn/
school fair /ˈskuːl feə/

1.3

Other

day off /ˌdeɪ ˈɒf/
tiring /ˈtaɪərɪŋ/

1.4

Communication

Asking for and offering help

Asking for help
Can you help me with the sofa, please?
Can you move the coffee table, please?

Reacting
I'm sorry, I can't. I'm busy right now.
No problem.
Yes, of course.

Offering help
Can I help you with the lamp?
Do you need any help with the lamp?

Reacting
No, that's fine, thank you.
Yes, please.

Other

ingredients /ɪnˈgriːdiənts/

1.5

Vocabulary

Personality adjectives

bossy /ˈbɒsi/
easy-going /ˌiːzi ˈgəʊɪŋ/
loud /laʊd/
messy /ˈmesi/
organised /ˈɔːgənaɪzd/
patient /ˈpeɪʃənt/
quiet /ˈkwaɪət/
tidy /ˈtaɪdi/

Other

argue about /ˌɑːgjuː əˈbaʊt/
bowl /bəʊl/
difficult /ˈdɪfɪkəlt/
easily /ˈiːzəli/
get upset /ˌget ʌpˈset/
lucky /ˈlʌki/
only child /ˌəʊnli ˈtʃaɪld/

Get Culture
Unusual places to live

above /əˈbʌv/
climate /ˈklaɪmət/
cover /ˈkʌvə/
for this reason /fə ˈðɪs ˌriːzən/
get light /ˌget ˈlaɪt/
glow-in-the-dark /ˌgləʊ ɪn ðə ˈdɑːk/
golf course /ˈgɒlf kɔːs/
grass /grɑːs/
igloo /ˈɪgluː/
in the east/north/south/west of /ɪn ði ˈiːst əv / ɪn ðə ˈnɔːθ əv / ɪn ðə ˈsaʊθ əv / ɪn ðə ˈwest əv/
last /lɑːst/
lose golf balls /ˌluːz ˈgɒlf bɔːlz/
on the coast /ɒn ðə ˈkəʊst/
percent /pəˈsent/
rain forest /ˈreɪn ˌfɒrɪst/
season /ˈsiːzən/
storm /stɔːm/
under the ground /ˌʌndə ðə ˈgraʊnd/

Word list

Unit 2
Shopping

2.1

Vocabulary
Shopping

Nouns
cashier /kæ'ʃɪə/
shopping bag /'ʃɒpɪŋ bæg/
shopping basket /'ʃɒpɪŋ ˌbɑ:skɪt/
shopping list /'ʃɒpɪŋ ˌlɪst/
shopping trolley /'ʃɒpɪŋ ˌtrɒli/
special offer /ˌspeʃəl 'ɒfə/

Phrases
carry the shopping /ˌkæri ðə 'ʃɒpɪŋ/
check the price /ˌtʃek ðə 'praɪs/
get a receipt /ˌget ə rɪ'si:t/
get your change /ˌget jə 'tʃeɪndʒ/
pay by card /ˌpeɪ baɪ 'kɑ:d/
pay for the shopping /ˌpeɪ fə ðə 'ʃɒpɪŋ/
pay in cash /ˌpeɪ ɪn 'kæʃ/
stand in a queue /ˌstænd ɪn ə 'kju:/

2.2

Say it!
Have fun! /ˌhæv 'fʌn/
Here we are! /ˌhɪə ˌwi: 'ɑ:/
I don't believe it! /ˌaɪ ˌdəʊnt bə'li:v ɪt/

Other
choose /tʃu:z/
hole /həʊl/
site /saɪt/
stylish /'staɪlɪʃ/

2.3

Vocabulary
Shops
baker's /'beɪkəz/
bookshop /'bʊkʃɒp/
chemist's /'keməsts/
clothes shop /'kləʊðz ʃɒp/
department store /dɪ'pɑ:tmənt stɔ:/
greengrocer's /'gri:nˌgrəʊsəz/
newsagent's /'nju:zˌeɪdʒənts/
shoe shop /'ʃu: ʃɒp/
sports shop /'spɔ:ts ʃɒp/

2.4

Communication
Shopping for clothes

Shop assistant
Can I help you?
Sorry, we don't.
The changing rooms are over there.
What size are you?
Yes, we do. Here you are.

Customer
Can I try it on?
Can I try them on?
Do you have this in grey?
Do you have these in grey?
Do you have this in a size 10 / in a small?
Do you have these in a size 10 / in a small?
I'm a size 10 / a small / a medium / a large.
I'm looking for new jeans.
No thanks, I'm just looking.

2.5

Other
book /bʊk/
brilliant /'brɪljənt/
cost /kɒst/
free /fri:/
make sure /ˌmeɪk 'ʃɔ:/
opening hours /'əʊpənɪŋ ˌaʊəz/
per person /pə 'pɜ:sən/
serve /sɜ:v/
snack /snæk/
staff /stɑ:f/
touch /tʌtʃ/
while /waɪl/

2.6

Writing
Ordering arguments
Finally /'faɪnəli/
First of all /'fɜ:st əv ˌɔ:l/
What's more /wɒts 'mɔ:/

Other
choice /tʃɔɪs/
design /dɪ'zaɪn/
portable charger /ˌpɔ:təbəl 'tʃɑ:dʒə/
portable speakers /ˌpɔ:təbəl 'spi:kəz/

Unit 3
Going on holiday

3.1

Vocabulary
Going on holiday
explore an area /ɪkˌsplɔ:r ən 'eəriə/
explore a city /ɪkˌsplɔ:r ə 'sɪti/
explore a town /ɪkˌsplɔ:r ə 'taʊn/
go camping /ˌgəʊ 'kæmpɪŋ/
go cycling /ˌgəʊ 'saɪklɪŋ/
go hiking /ˌgəʊ 'haɪkɪŋ/
go on a boat trip /ˌgəʊ ɒn ə 'bəʊt trɪp/
go on a day trip /ˌgəʊ ɒn ə 'deɪ trɪp/
go on a guided tour /ˌgəʊ ɒn ə ˌgaɪdɪd 'tʊə/
go snorkelling /ˌgəʊ 'snɔ:kəlɪŋ/
go to the beach /ˌgəʊ tə ðə 'bi:tʃ/
try the local food /ˌtraɪ ðə ˌləʊkəl 'fu:d/

3.2

Say it!
That's weird! /ˌðæts 'wɪəd/
What on earth ...? /ˌwɒt ɒn 'ɜ:θ/

Other
a week ago /ə ˌwi:k ə'gəʊ/
airport /'eəpɔ:t/
catch /kætʃ/
give me a hand /ˌgɪv mi ə 'hænd/
lock the back door /ˌlɒk ðə ˌbæk 'dɔ:/
pillow /'pɪləʊ/
still /stɪl/

3.3

Other
Pleased to meet you. /ˌpli:zd tə 'mi:t jə/
premiere /'premieə/

3.4

Communication
Requests

Making requests
Can I have the tablet?
Can you bring me my phone, please?
Could you give me the key to my room?

Responding to requests
Not now, sorry. I'm busy.
Sorry, you can't. / Sorry, I can't. I'm using it right now.
Yes, no problem.
Yes, of course.

Other
train timetable /ˌtreɪn 'taɪmˌteɪbəl/
lend /lend/
souvenir /ˌsu:və'nɪə/

3.5

Vocabulary
Phrases with *get*
get bored /ˌget 'bɔ:d/
get cold /ˌget 'kəʊld/
get dark /ˌget 'dɑ:k/
get lost /ˌget 'lɒst/
get tired /ˌget 'taɪəd/

Other
caravan /'kærəvæn/
go fishing /ˌgəʊ 'fɪʃɪŋ/
grizzly bears /'grɪzli beəz/
have a rest /ˌhæv ə 'rest/
humpback whales /ˌhʌmpbæk 'weɪlz/
lazy /'leɪzi/
state /steɪt/
wolf /wʊlf/

3.6

Other
fit /fɪt/
for hours /fər 'aʊəz/

Get Culture
A journey around the USA
geyser /'gi:zə/
landscape /'lændskeɪp/
make up /ˌmeɪk 'ʌp/
neighbours /'neɪbəz/
main /meɪn/
wetlands /'wetləndz/

Unit 4
Useful things

4.1

Vocabulary
Useful things
blender /'blendə/
DVD player /ˌdi:vi: 'di: ˌpleɪə/
electric toothbrush /ɪˌlektrɪk 'tu:θbrʌʃ/
games console /'geɪmz 'kɒnsəʊl/
hairdryer /'heəˌdraɪə/
microwave oven /ˌmaɪkrəweɪv 'ʌvən/
remote control /rɪˌməʊt kən'trəʊl/
smart TV /ˌsmɑ:t ˌti:'vi:/
toaster /'təʊstə/
USB stick /ˌju: es 'bi: stɪk/

Vocabulary
Using technology
plug in /ˌplʌg 'ɪn/
turn off /ˌtɜ:n 'ɒf/
turn on /ˌtɜ:n 'ɒn/
unplug /ʌn'plʌg/

Other
do a survey /ˌdu: ə 'sɜ:veɪ/
press /pres/

4.2

Say it!
Check this out! /ˌtʃek ðɪs 'aʊt/
Honest! /'ɒnɪst/
You're kidding! /ˌjə 'kɪdɪŋ/

Other
board game /'bɔ:d geɪm/
film crew /'fɪlm kru:/

4.3

Other
break /breɪk/
button /'bʌtn/
invent /ɪn'vent/
invention /ɪn'venʃən/
postman /'pəʊstmən/
push /pʊʃ/
snack maker /'snæk ˌmeɪkə/
storm /stɔ:m/

4.4

Communication
Sympathising

Asking what happened
What happened?
What's wrong?
You look upset.
You look worried.

Reacting to bad news
I'm sorry to hear that!

Oh, that's terrible!
That's a shame.
Other
drop /drɒp/
dry my hair /ˌdraɪ maɪ 'heə/
Lucky you! /ˌlʌki 'juː/
miss the bus /ˌmɪs ðə 'bʌs/
repair /rɪ'peə/

4.5

Vocabulary

Smartphones

app /æp/
battery /'bætəri/
portable charger /ˌpɔːtəbəl 'tʃɑːdʒə/
ringtone /'rɪŋtəʊn/
touch screen /'tʌtʃ skriːn/
Wi-Fi /'waɪfaɪ/
Other
cell phone /'sel fəʊn/
connect /kə'nekt/
different from /'dɪfərənt frəm/
hand-held /'hænd held/
last /lɑːst/
mobile phone call /ˌməʊbaɪl ˌfəʊn 'kɔːl/
office /'ɒfɪs/
rival company /ˌraɪvəl 'kʌmpəni/
weigh /weɪ/
work for /'wɜːk fə/

4.6

Other
be late /ˌbi 'leɪt/
get on a bus /ˌget ɒn ə 'bʌs/
main event /ˌmeɪn ɪ'vent/

Writing

Using past tenses in a story

Finally /'faɪnəli/
First /fɜːst/
Then /ðen/

Unit 5
Health matters

5.1

Vocabulary

Health problems

Nouns
a blocked nose /ə ˌblɒkt 'nəʊz/
a cold /ə 'kəʊld/
a cough /ə 'kɒf/
earache /'ɪəreɪk/
a headache /ə 'hedeɪk/
a runny nose /ə ˌrʌni 'nəʊz/
a sore throat /ə ˌsɔː 'θrəʊt/
a stomachache /ə 'stʌməkeɪk/
a temperature /ə 'temprətʃə/
toothache /'tuːθeɪk/
Verbs
cough /kɒf/
sneeze /sniːz/

5.2

Say it!
Get well soon! /ˌget ˌwel 'suːn/
It's me again. /ˌɪts 'miː əˌgen/
See you soon! /ˌsiː jə 'suːn/
Other
at least /ət 'liːst/
flu /fluː/
pick up /ˌpɪk 'ʌp/
practice /'præktɪs/
practise /'præktɪs/

5.3

Vocabulary

Injuries

broken leg /ˌbrəʊkən 'leg/
bruise /bruːz/
burn /bɜːn/
cut /kʌt/
mosquito bite /mə'skiːtəʊ baɪt/
Other
call an ambulance /ˌkɔːl ən 'æmbjələns/
lie down /ˌlaɪ 'daʊn/
mosquito net /mə'skiːtəʊ net/
move /muːv/
nasty /'nɑːsti/

5.4

Communication

Giving health advice

Asking about health
What's wrong?
What's the matter?
Responding
I don't feel very well.
I feel terrible.
I've got a cut.
I've got a headache.
Giving advice
I think you should see the doctor/dentist.
Put a plaster on it.
Put some cream on it.
Put some ice on it.
Why don't you drink some mint tea?
Why don't you lie down?
Why don't you take a painkiller?
Accepting advice
Yes, that's a good idea.
Yes, you're right.
Other
stomach /'stʌmək/
sweetheart /'swiːthɑːt/
The test is off. /ðə ˌtest ɪz 'ɒf/

5.5

Vocabulary

The body

blood /blʌd/
bones /bəʊnz/
brain /breɪn/
heart /hɑːt/
muscles /'mʌsəls/

Other
become weaker /bɪˌkʌm 'wiːkə/
exactly /ɪg'zæktli/
find out /ˌfaɪnd 'aʊt/
get fit /ˌget' fɪt/
get ill /ˌget 'ɪl/
get old /ˌget 'əʊld/
rest /rest/
strong /strɒŋ/
the heart beats /ðə ˌhɑːt 'biːts/

5.6

Other
coach /kəʊtʃ/
collect money /kəˌlekt 'mʌni/
do a warm-up /ˌduː ə 'wɔːm ʌp/
for charity /fə 'tʃærəti/
get strong /ˌget 'strɒŋ/
mind /maɪnd/
take a snack /ˌteɪk ə 'snæk/

Get Culture
British TV

broadcast /'brɔːdkɑːst/
care for /'keə fə/
documentary /ˌdɒkjə'mentəri/
game show /'geɪm ʃəʊ/
natural environment /ˌnætʃərəl ɪn'vaɪrənmənt/
news /njuːz/
protect /prə'tekt/
sitcom /'sɪtkɒm/
soap opera /'səʊp ˌɒpərə/
talent show /'tælənt ʃəʊ/
TV series /ˌtiːˌviː 'sɪəriːz/
viewer /'vjuːə/

Unit 6
Cooking and eating

6.1

Vocabulary

Cooking verbs

add /æd/
bake /beɪk/
beat /biːt/
boil /bɔɪl/
chop /tʃɒp/
fry /fraɪ/
mix /mɪks/
peel /piːl/
roast /rəʊst/
slice /slaɪs/

Vocabulary

Cooking nouns

bowl /bəʊl/
cake tin /'keɪk tɪn/
frying pan /'fraɪɪŋ pæn/
oven /'ʌvən/
pot /pɒt/
Other
cocoa /'kəʊkəʊ/
dessert /dɪ'zɜːt/
dish /dɪʃ/
garlic /'gɑːlɪk/

onions /'ʌnjənz/
salt /sɔːlt/
sauce /sɔːs/
take a course /ˌteɪk ə 'kɔːs/

6.2

Say it!
I'm starving! /aɪm 'stɑːvɪŋ/
Let's have a look. /ˌlets həv ə 'lʊk/
What's next? /ˌwɒts 'nekst/

Vocabulary

Serving and eating food

cup /kʌp/
fork /fɔːk/
glass /glɑːs/
knife /naɪf/
mug /mʌg/
plate /pleɪt/
spoon /spuːn/
Other
chicken pie /ˌtʃɪkɪn 'paɪ/
cupboard /'kʌbəd/

6.3

Other
corn /kɔːn/
cover the pot /ˌkʌvə ðə 'pɒt/
take off the coat /teɪk ˌɒf ðə 'kəʊt/
win a singing competition /wɪn ə 'sɪŋɪŋ ˌkɒmpəˌtɪʃən/

6.4

Communication

Preferences

Asking about preferences
Would you like to have a picnic or go for a bike ride?
Would you like cheese or tuna?
Responding
I'd like to go for a bike ride.
I'd like cheese.
I don't mind.
I'd prefer cheese.
You choose.
Other
How about something sweet? /haʊ əˌbaʊt ˌsʌmθɪŋ 'swiːt/

6.5

Vocabulary

Describing food

delicious /dɪ'lɪʃəs/
disgusting /dis'gʌstɪŋ/
salty /'sɔːlti/
sour /'saʊə/
spicy /'spaɪsi/
sweet /swiːt/
Other
ancient Romans /ˌeɪnʃənt 'rəʊmənz/
charcoal /'tʃɑːkəʊl/
flavour /'fleɪvə/
freeze /friːz/

Word list

honey /ˈhʌni/
rich /rɪtʃ/
smelly /ˈsmeli/

6.6

Other

sharp /ʃɑːp/

Unit 7
Where I live

7.1

Vocabulary
Places to live

Types of houses

block of flats /ˌblɒk əv ˈflæts/
cottage /ˈkɒtɪdʒ/
detached house /dɪˈtætʃt haʊs/
flat /flæt/
semi-detached house /ˌsemi dɪˈtætʃt haʊs/
terraced house /ˈterɪst haʊs/

Location

in a city /ɪn ə ˈsɪti/
in a town /ɪn ə ˈtaʊn/
in a village /ɪn ə ˈvɪlɪdʒ/
in the country /ɪn ðə ˈkʌntri/
on an island /ɒn ən ˈaɪlənd/

Vocabulary
Parts of the house

attic /ˈætɪk/
balcony /ˈbælkəni/
basement /ˈbeɪsmənt/
first floor /ˌfɜːst ˈflɔː/
ground floor /ˌɡraʊnd ˈflɔː/
lift /lɪft/
stairs /steəz/
top floor /ˌtɒp ˈflɔː/

Other

I never walk up the stairs. /aɪ ˌnevə ˌwɔːk ʌp ðə ˈsteəz/
I use the lift to go up. /aɪ ˌjuːz ðə ˌlɪft tə ɡəʊ ˈʌp/

7.2

Say it!

It depends. /ɪt dɪˈpendz/
Remember? /rɪˈmembə/
See you later! /ˌsiː jə ˈleɪtə/

Other

catch the bus /ˌkætʃ ðə ˈbʌs/
future /ˈfjuːtʃə/
go on a business trip /ˌɡəʊ ɒn ə ˈbɪznəs trɪp/
in a hurry /ɪn ə ˈhʌri/
in five minutes /ɪn ˌfaɪv ˈmɪnəts/
next week /ˌnekst ˈwiːk/
Pick me up. /ˌpɪk mi ˈʌp/
this evening /ðɪs ˈiːvnɪŋ/
tidy the garden /ˌtaɪdi ðə ˈɡɑːdn/
tomorrow evening /təˌmɒrəʊ ˈiːvnɪŋ/
We're moving house. /wɪə ˌmuːvɪŋ ˈhaʊs/

7.3

Vocabulary
In the house

bookcase /ˈbʊkkeɪs/
cupboard /ˈkʌbəd/
drawer /drɔː/
mirror /ˈmɪrə/
sink /sɪŋk/
tap /tæp/

Other

house rules /ˈhaʊs ruːlz/
immediately /ɪˈmiːdiətli/
leave /liːv/
make a mess /ˌmeɪk ə ˈmes/
put things away /ˌpʊt θɪŋz əˈweɪ/
sticker /ˈstɪkə/

7.4

Communication
Invitations

Making an invitation

Are you free on Sunday? Would you like to hang out?
Do you want to hang out on Sunday?
Mum's taking us to the adventure park on Saturday. Can you come?

Accepting an invitation

That sounds fun. Thank you.
That sounds great. Thank you.
Yes, I'd love to, thanks.

Declining an invitation

I'd love to, but we're visiting our cousins this Saturday.
I'm sorry, I can't (come). I'm busy on Saturday.
Sorry, maybe next time.

7.5

Vocabulary
Phrasal verbs

check out /ˌtʃek ˈaʊt/
clean up /ˌkliːn ˈʌp/
find out /ˌfaɪnd ˈaʊt/
look for /ˌlʊk ˈfɔː/
wake up /ˌweɪk ˈʌp/

Other

awful /ˈɔːfəl/
bird bath /ˈbɜːd bɑːθ/
Clean up after your dog. /ˌkliːn ˌʌp ˌɑːftə jə ˈdɒɡ/
drop litter /ˌdrɒp ˈlɪtə/
expect /ɪkˈspekt/
flower pot /ˈflaʊə pɒt/
ground /ɡraʊnd/
neighbourhood /ˈneɪbəhʊd/
plant flowers /ˌplɑːnt ˈflaʊəz/
though /ðəʊ/
useful /ˈjuːsfəl/

7.6

Other

gate /ɡeɪt/
It's a great way to meet our neighbours. /ɪts ə ˌɡreɪt ˌweɪ tə ˌmiːt aʊə ˈneɪbəz/
switch off /ˌswɪtʃ ˈɒf/

Get Culture
Very British food

cracker /ˈkrækə/
It comes in many flavours and colours. /ɪt ˌkʌmz ɪn ˌmeni ˌfleɪvəz ənd ˈkʌləz/
mixture /ˈmɪkstʃə/
mustard /ˈmʌstəd/
pie /paɪ/
seaside /ˈsiːsaɪd/
share /ʃeə/
shortbread /ˈʃɔːtbred/
simple /ˈsɪmpəl/
takeaway food /ˈteɪkəweɪ fuːd/
tasty /ˈteɪsti/
Welsh /welʃ/
Yorkshire pudding /ˌjɔːkʃə ˈpʊdɪŋ/

Unit 8
A happy life

8.1

Vocabulary
Life ambitions

be a doctor /ˌbi ə ˈdɒktə/
be famous /ˌbi ˈfeɪməs/
be rich /ˌbi ˈrɪtʃ/
have a family /ˌhæv ə ˈfæməli/
have an interesting job /ˌhæv ən ˌɪntrəstɪŋ ˈdʒɒb/
have my own business /ˌhæv maɪ əʊn ˈbɪznəs/
learn a foreign language /ˌlɜːn ə ˌfɒrɪn ˈlæŋɡwɪdʒ/
learn to drive /ˌlɜːn tə ˈdraɪv/
live abroad /ˌlɪv əˈbrɔːd/
live on my own /ˌlɪv ɒn maɪ ˈəʊn/

Other

husband /ˈhʌzbənd/
perhaps /pəˈhæps/

8.2

Say it!

Here's a thought. /hɪəz ə θɔːt/
It's hard to decide. /ɪts ˌhɑːd tə dɪˈsaɪd/
My turn now. /ˈmaɪ ˌtɜːn naʊ/

Other

share a room /ʃeər ə ˈruːm/
snore like a hippo /ˌsnɔː laɪk ə ˈhɪpəʊ/

8.3

Vocabulary
Being with people

call /kɔːl/
give someone a hug /ˌɡɪv ˌsʌmwʌn ə ˈhʌɡ/
invite /ɪnˈvaɪt/
kiss /kɪs/
shake hands /ˌʃeɪk ˈhændz/
visit /ˈvɪzɪt/

8.4

Communication
Agreeing and disagreeing

Agreeing

I agree (with you).
That's right.
That's true.
That's what I think too.
You're right.

Disagreeing

I disagree (with you).
I don't agree (with you).
I don't think so.
That isn't right.
That's not true.
You're wrong.

Other

give someone a headache /ˌɡɪv ˌsʌmwʌn ə ˈhedeɪk/
on the radio /ˌɒn ðə ˈreɪdiəʊ/
second-hand /ˌsekənd ˈhænd/
turn the music down /ˌtɜːn ðə ˌmjuːzɪk ˈdaʊn/

8.5

Vocabulary
Good manners

arrive on time /əˌraɪv ɒn ˈtaɪm/
ask for permission /ˌɑːsk fə pəˈmɪʃən/
be late /ˌbi ˈleɪt/
be polite /ˌbi pəˈlaɪt/
interrupt /ˌɪntəˈrʌpt/
wait your turn /ˌweɪt jə ˈtɜːn/

Other

annoying /əˈnɔɪɪŋ/
care about /ˌkeər əˈbaʊt/
common /ˈkɒmən/
complain /ˌkəmˈpleɪn/
explain something to someone /ɪkˈspleɪn ˌsʌmθɪŋ tə ˌsʌmwʌn/
keep someone waiting /ˌkiːp ˌsʌmwʌn ˈweɪtɪŋ/

8.6

Other

everybody /ˈevribɒdi/
ride a bicycle /ˌraɪd ə ˈbaɪsɪkəl/

Irregular verbs

Infinitive	Past Simple	Past Participle
be /bɪː/	was/were /wɒz/wɜː/	been /bɪːn/
become /bɪ'kʌm/	became /bɪ'keɪm/	become /bɪ'kʌm/
break /breɪk/	broke /brəʊk/	broken /'brəʊkən/
bring /brɪŋ/	brought /brɔːt/	brought /brɔːt/
build /bɪld/	built /bɪlt/	built /bɪlt/
buy /baɪ/	bought /bɔːt/	bought /bɔːt/
catch /kætʃ/	caught /kɔːt/	caught /kɔːt/
choose /tʃʊːz/	chose /tʃəʊz/	chosen /'tʃəʊzn/
come /kʌm/	came /keɪm/	come /kʌm/
cost /kɒst/	cost /kɒst/	cost /kɒst/
cut /kʌt/	cut /kʌt/	cut /kʌt/
do /dʊː/	did /dɪd/	done /dʌn/
draw /drɔː/	drew /drʊː/	drawn /drɔːn/
dream /drɪːm/	dreamed /drɪːmd/ dreamt /dremt/	dreamed /drɪːmd/ dreamt /dremt/
drink /drɪnk/	drank /drænk/	drunk /drʌnk/
drive /draɪv/	drove /drəʊv/	driven /'drɪvn/
eat /ɪːt/	ate /et/	eaten /'ɪːtn/
fall /fɔːl/	fell /fel/	fallen /'fɔːln/
feed /fɪːd/	fed /fed/	fed /fed/
feel /fɪːl/	felt /felt/	felt /felt/
find /faɪnd/	found /faʊnd/	found /faʊnd/
fly /flaɪ/	flew /flʊː/	flown /fləʊn/
forget /fə'get/	forgot /fə'gɒt/	forgotten /fə'gɒtn/
get /get/	got /gɒt/	got /gɒt/
give /gɪv/	gave /geɪv/	given /'gɪvn/
go /gəʊ/	went /went/	gone /gɒn/
grow /grəʊ/	grew /grʊː/	grown /grəʊn/
hang /hæŋ/	hung /hʌŋ/	hung /hʌŋ/
have /hæv/	had /hæd/	had /hæd/
hear /hɪə/	heard /hɜːd/	heard /hɜːd/
keep /kɪːp/	kept /kept/	kept /kept/
know /nəʊ/	knew /njʊː/	known /nəʊn/
learn /lɜːn/	learned /lɜːnd/ learnt /lɜːnt/	learned /lɜːnd/ learnt /lɜːnt/

Infinitive	Past Simple	Past Participle
leave /lɪːv/	left /left/	left /left/
lend /lend/	lent /lent/	lent /lent/
lie /laɪ/	lay /leɪ/	lain /leɪn/
lose /lʊːz/	lost /lɒst/	lost /lɒst/
make /meɪk/	made /meɪd/	made /meɪd/
meet /mɪːt/	met /met/	met /met/
pay /peɪ/	paid /peɪd/	paid /peɪd/
put /pʊt/	put /pʊt/	put /pʊt/
read /rɪːd/	read /red/	read /red/
ride /raɪd/	rode /rəʊd/	ridden /'rɪdn/
run /rʌn/	ran /ræn/	run /rʌn/
say /seɪ/	said /sed/	said /sed/
see /sɪː/	saw /sɔː/	seen /sɪːn/
send /send/	sent /sent/	sent /sent/
set /set/	set /set/	set /set/
sing /sɪŋ/	sang /sæŋ/	sung /sʌŋ/
sit /sɪt/	sat /sæt/	sat /sæt/
sleep /slɪːp/	slept /slept/	slept /slept/
speak /spɪːk/	spoke /spəʊk/	spoken /'spəʊkən/
spend /spend/	spent /spent/	spent /spent/
spell /spel/	spelt /spelt/ spelled /speld/	spelt /spelt/ spelled /speld/
stand /stæŋd/	stood /stʊd/	stood /stʊd/
swim /swɪm/	swam /swæm/	swum /swʌm/
take /teɪk/	took /tʊk/	taken /'teɪkən/
tell /tel/	told /təʊld/	told /təʊld/
think /θɪnk/	thought /θɔːt/	thought /θɔːt/
throw /θrəʊ/	threw /θruː/	thrown / θrəʊn/
understand /ˌʌndə'stænd/	understood /ˌʌndə'stʊd/	understood /ˌʌndə'stʊd/
wake /weɪk/	woke /wəʊk/	woken /'wəʊkən/
wear /weə/	wore /wɔː/	worn /wɔːn/
win /wɪn/	won /wʌn/	won /wʌn/
write /raɪt/	wrote /rəʊt/	written /'rɪtn/

Student B activities

Unit 1 Lesson 1.2, Page 13, Exercise 10

Find differences between your picture and Student A's picture.

1 Listen to Student A. Is the same thing or a different thing happening in your picture?

A: *In my picture, the man is ironing.*

B: *Yes, in my picture, he's ironing too.*

2 What's happening in your picture? Tell Student A using the verbs in the box.

feed listen set

B: *In my picture, the woman is …* A: *In my picture, she's …*

Unit 5 Lesson 5.3, Page 63, Exercise 7

1 Ask Student A this question. Listen and complete the notes.

B: *What should I do to prevent mosquito bites?*

Going camping? Here's how to prevent mosquito bites:

- camp near [1] __________ ✗
- wear [2] __________ colours ✓
- wear [3] __________ and T-shirts ✗
- use a [4] __________ ✓

2 Answer Student A's question. Use the information in the leaflet.

Going camping? Here's how to prevent burns:

- go near the fire ✗
- build the fire far away from the tent ✓
- touch hot pots and pans ✗
- have some water near the fire ✓

B: *You shouldn't go near the fire.*

Student A&B activities

Unit 6 Lesson 6.6, Page 78, Exercise 6

1 __________ and chop one onion.

2 __________ two tomatoes.

3 __________ the onion.

4 __________ the tomatoes, and some salt and pepper.

5 __________ some pasta.

6 Put the sauce on the pasta.

Unit 8 Lesson 8.4, Page 100, Exercise 5

1 Complete the list with your opinions.

1 the best music: __________
2 a great computer game: __________
3 a good book: __________
4 a fun hobby: __________
5 an exciting sport: __________
6 delicious food: __________

2 In pairs, take turns to say what you think. Your partner can agree or disagree.

A: *I think that rap is the best music.*

B: *I don't think so. I think rock is better.*